BLOODSUCKERS

ON THE

BAYOU

Other Works by Valerie Estelle Frankel

Henry Potty and the Pet Rock: An Unauthorized Harry Potter Parody

Henry Potty and the Deathly Paper Shortage: An Unauthorized Harry Potter Parody

Buffy and the Heroine's Journey

From Girl to Goddess: The Heroine's Journey in Myth and Legend

Katniss the Cattail: An Unauthorized Guide to Names and Symbols in The Hunger Games

The Many Faces of Katniss Everdeen: Exploring the Heroine of The Hunger Games

Harry Potter, Still Recruiting: An Inner Look at Harry Potter Fandom

An Unexpected Parody: The Unauthorized Spoof of The Hobbit Movie

Teaching with Harry Potter

Myths and Motifs in The Mortal Instruments

Winning the Game of Thrones: The Host of Characters and their Agendas

Winter is Coming: Symbols, Portents, and Hidden Meanings in A Game of Thrones

BLOODSUCKERS

ON THE

BAYOU

The Myths, Symbols, &

Tales Behind

HBO's

TRUE BLOOD

LitCrit Press
ISBN 13: 978-0615857800

ISBN-10: 0615857809

Contents

With a special thanks to Matt Gottlieb, who told me my formatting was off and kept saying it until I paid attention.

Introduction

In 2001, Southern author Charlaine Harris sold her first Sookie Stackhouse novel. It was the latest of several mystery series, as when she had married her second husband in 1978, he presented her with a typewriter and encouraged her to follow her dream. She published her first novel, the mystery *Sweet and Deadly*, in 1981.

The Aurora Teagarden and Lily Bard series soon followed, featuring a Georgia librarian and a cleaning lady from Arkansas who each solve local mysteries. *Dead Until Dark*, the first Sookie Stackhouse novel, built heavily on these and was intended for a similar audience. At the same time, it dipped into the supernatural with vampires and shifters, with other paranormal creatures to follow. As a reaction to Anne Rice's New Orleans vampires, Harris thought, "Wouldn't it be funny to take the very prosaic, unromantic *northern* part of Louisiana and put my vampires there?" (Wilcott 27). As a genre-crossing Southern urban paranormal fantasy-mystery, it quickly developed an enthusiastic fanbase.

While early for a dentist appointment, producer Alan Ball was browsing through Barnes and Noble and came across *Dead Until Dark*. As he read more of the series, he expressed an interest in adapting the books for television. Though he lives and works in Los Angeles, he hails from Marietta, Georgia, and quickly vibed with the portrayal of Southern gothic.

Having created, written, and produced the HBO series *Six Feet Under*, he was following the success of his academy award winning film *American Beauty* and critically acclaimed

11

independent film *Towelhead.* Describing *Six Feet Under,* Anna
Paquin, who plays Sookie on the show, notes,

> I've seen every episode at least two or three times. I love
> how real all of those relationships are, and how he depicts
> families but also weaves in these odd elements, like the
> figure of the dead father, in a way that's not cheesy or
> crazy. He can make you believe things even if they're not
> 100 percent based in reality. When he's directing or on set,
> he's like the favorite parent. It's like *Everybody Loves Alan.*
> Even if it's 4 A.M. and everyone's covered in mud and blood
> and whatever, he still keeps everyone having a good time.
> (Martin)

While Harris had other offers, she notes, "He understood
what the books were about, a mixture of extremes: humor,
violence, awakenings" (Wilcott 27). Ball in turn admires Harris's
profound statements about the culture "wrapped up in a fun
amusement-park, gothic, romantic, science-fiction slasher
movie" (Wilcott 21).

True Blood premiered on September 7, 2008 on HBO. That
September, after only the first two episodes had aired, HBO
placed an order for a second season of twelve episodes, and the
show took off. Now the show is in its sixth season, with seven
optioned, with Brian Buckner replacing Ball as the showrunner
Meanwhile, the book series continued, even as they diverged
wildly, and finished with the thirteenth book in May 2013, as
Sookie solves her final crime and settles down with her true
love. "I do feel a responsibility to be true to her world," Ball
notes, and the spirit of characters like Eric, Jason, and sweet,
perky Sookie certainly lives on, even if the plots are different.

This book explores the mythic patterns buried inside
Sookie's tale, as she, like countless epic heroines before her,
faces villains who represent her dark side, descends into death,
and grows through the journey. Her friends represent parts of
her personality, from saucy Pam to trickster Eric. This is mostly
an exploration of the show, using tidbits from the books, but
not relying on book knowledge or blasting the reader with
dreaded "spoilers."

On the show more than in the books, the other characters undergo epic quests and growth through facing their neglected dark sides. Sam deals with his younger self, personified by his brother Tommy, and Alcide defeats bad packmasters to become a good one. Tara studies with mentors who represent female hedonism (Maryann the Maenad) and female rage (Marnie the Wiccan) as she struggle to channel her own ostracized resentment. Lafayette explores the magic within himself, and Jason searches for adulthood.

It's not surprising the series deals with the classic hero's and heroine's journey, as it incorporates much classical mythology. Of course, vampires, fairies, werewolves, and even were-panthers come from ancient sources and are rendered somewhat traditionally, with ancient texts presented her for comparison. This book likewise offers background on maenads and ifrit, the brujo tradition and Lilith worship.

Books vs Show
"For the 'book-ies' out there, everyone has to remember that it's an adaptation, not a translation," Alan Ball explains (O'Connor). Indeed, there are many differences. Book fans have seen the show drift further and further after the first two episodes, until the plots of season five and six are basically unrecognizable from the books.

Season one is closest: Book Sookie must find the man who murders waitresses who are also Jason's hookups. Her grandmother is murdered before she discovers René is the culprit. Meanwhile, Sookie saves Bill from the Rattrays and they fall in love.

In season two as well as book two, Eric hires Sookie to accompany him to Dallas and finally infiltrate the Church of the Sun. Book Jason is not a participant in the plot, and never joins the church. Godric meets the sun, but he's a random vampire, not Eric's beloved maker. Otherwise, this plot is similar. The maenad, however, is a very minor character that Sam dates while Tara is dating a pleasant, rather conventional man named Eggs. That's about as far as the book-plot is developed.

The season three plot—Russell Edgington and Lorena have

captured Bill, and Sookie and Alcide must free him—is similar in the book. Tara's Franklin isn't bad, but he soon "passes her on" to a violent vampire creep. In book four, Eric's amnesia from a witch coven and his love for Sookie are similar, as is the battle with the coven. In the following books, there's no sign of Lilith, vampire Authority, Vampire Bible, vampire religion, or torture camp for vampires. Vampires are mainstreaming successfully, and the weres and shifters come out as well.

Sookie then travels to a vampire summit as Queen Sophie-Ann's assistant. When disaster strikes (then Katrina strikes!) and a wounded Sophie-Ann is replaced, Eric must struggle to remain sheriff and find a way to win over Sookie. Alcide becomes packmaster after his father dies struggling to do the same, but no one's taking V or making deals with a surprisingly banal Russell Edgington.

Niall, Sookie's fairy great-grandfather, does arrive in time for a fairy war between his faction, which cares for humans, and another, which believes halfbreeds like Sookie are an abomination. Claudine, Sookie's fairy godmother, and her brother Claude seek to protect her. While Sookie survives the war, she's tortured by evil fairies and comes out wounded and traumatized. Several of her fairy relatives from the strip club move in with her and become major characters, though again, there isn't a great deal of plot arc.

Basically each book begins with a mysterious murder or violent event, all of which Sookie must unravel with her life on the line and terror escalating. Often the culprit is someone close to her that she trusted.

The books are Sookie's tale as she struggles to find love. As such, she tries many paranormal relationships as she decides whom she wants to spend her life with. There's Alcide the werewolf, Quinn the were-tiger, Calvin the were-panther, and of course Eric and Bill. Sam is a younger, more serious contender. Harris says Sookie's taken a little away from ever relationship she's had as she grows toward a meaningful relationship with her final choice. "For someone who always thought it would be impossible to have a permanent relationship with someone, she learned she could" (Tyley, "Charlaine Harris on Death

Threats").

Other characters' plots are limited: Tara (with much less personality), Holly, Andy, Andy's sister Portia, and Hoyt have all settled down in conventional marriages with conventional spouses and barely feature in the plot. They don't have lengthy battles with hate groups, supernatural encounters, or drugs. Sam manages the bar, and doesn't have a deadbeat family, girlfriend Luna, or cause to fight for. Sam's family is much more prosaic, as is Tara's. Jason becomes a were-panther and marries twice, but his season four/book four plot takes place away from readers' view and is thus minimized. (On the show, Jason frequently wears a baseball cap with a panther on it, in reference to his book transformation.) Jessica never exists. Lafayette dies and is replaced by many interchangeable cooks. Terry is still bartending, and hasn't gotten a handle on the PTSD or gotten married (until the series end at least). Arlene is the one to get involved with Fellowship of the Sun and become a vampire-hater. Pam is still Pam, but with no vampire Tara or sister Nora, only her and Eric. Meanwhile, Bill is geekily working on a vampire database and struggling with depression as Sookie makes it clear she's no longer interested.

Various "Easter eggs" exist to amuse fans of book and show together. Charlaine Harris can be seen sitting at Merlotte's complaining after the chaos of the maenad. (2.12). In the first episode, Gran reads *Last Scene Alive*, a novel by Charlaine Harris. In season four's "If You Love Me, Why Am I Dyin?" likewise Sookie reads a Charlaine Harris novel. One of Andy's daughters is named Charlaine. In return, *Dead in the Family* opens with Jace Everett's "Bad Things" playing on the jukebox. Though the two series nod to each other, and begin on the same page, their character arcs are the most divergent.

BLOODSUCKERS ON THE BAYOU

The Heroine's Journey

As Joseph Campbell relates in his work on the hero's journey: "The hero feels something's lacking in his life. He then goes off to recover it or to discover a life-giving elixir. There's a cycle of going and returning" (Campbell and Moyers 123). This quest, into the otherworld of fairyland or the dark underworld of death, represents facing one's dark side and thus journeying into adulthood. It's the most popular story pattern for fantasy, creating the foundation of plots from *Harry Potter* to *Star Wars*.

The heroine's journey is similar, though not identical. The heroine is more likely to have a magical box (seen in the twelfth Sookie Stackhouse novel) or light (seen in the show's sixth season) rather than a hero sword, wand, or lightsaber.

> The heroine's friends augment her natural feminine insight with masculine rationality and order, while her lover is a shapeshifting monster of the magical world—a frog prince or beast-husband (or two-faced vampire!). The epic heroine wields a magic charm or prophetic mirror, not a sword. And she destroys murderers and their undead servants as the champion of life. As she struggles against the Patriarchy— the distant or unloving father—she grows into someone who creates her own destiny.
>
> Eventually, she too descends into the underworld in a maiden's white gown, there to die and be reborn greater than before. Awaiting her is the wicked stepmother or Terrible Mother (as Jung calls her): the White Witch of Narnia or Wicked Witch of the West, slayer of children and figure of sterility and unlife. This brutal matriarch is often her

only mentor. The heroine not only defeats her; she grows from the lesson and rejoins the world as young mother, queen, and eternal goddess. (Frankel, *Buffy* 6)

When Sookie faces an antagonist who represents her own dark side, it's the "wicked witches" Maryann, Lorena, and Marnie, all slayers of the innocent, rather than the hero's classic dark lord. The monsters she confronts "are the forces of fragmentation, self-loathing, fear, and paralysis" as metaphors brought to life (Pearson and Pope 63). She's on a mission to save and protect others like Lucy of the Narnia books or Katniss of *The Hunger Games*. Indeed, Sookie risks her life solving crimes, and puts all she has on the line when Bill is captured by Lorena or Tara is imprisoned by Marnie. Both times she walks into the darkest place of all and stares down death but emerges from her conflict stronger and more assured.

Campbell's Hero's Journey	Frankel's Heroine's Journey
The World of Common Day	The World of Common Day
The Call To Adventure	The Call To Adventure
Refusal of the Call	Refusal of the Call
Supernatural Aid	The Ruthless Mentor and the Bladeless Talisman
The Crossing of the First Threshold The Belly of the Whale	The Crossing of the First Threshold Opening One's Senses
The Road of Trials	Sidekicks, Trials, Adversaries
The Meeting With the Goddess Woman as the Temptress	Wedding the Animus Facing Bluebeard Finding the Sensitive Man Confronting the Powerless Father
Atonement with the Father Apotheosis	Descent into Darkness Atonement with the Mother Integration and Apotheosis
The Ultimate Boon	Reward: Winning the Family
Refusal of the Return The Magic Flight Rescue From Without The Crossing of the Return Threshold	Torn Desires The Magic Flight Reinstating the Family Return
Master of the Two Worlds	Power over Life and Death
Freedom To Live	Ascension of the New Mother

As the classic heroine faces death and returns from the journey, she grows into a leader and defender of her community. This Sookie does when she disappears into Fairyland at the end of season three. When she returns, she's strong, sassy and independent, with a new grasp of her powers. Eric summarizes her struggle perfectly:

> Eric: There are two Sookie Stackhouses. One who still clings to the idea that she's merely human, and the other who's coming to grips with the fact that you are better than that..
> Sookie: And what do you think's gonna happen when I do come to grips with it? Do you think my legs are just gonna magically open for you?
> Eric: Well, that was saucy. Must have been Faerie Sookie talking. I like when she comes out.
> Sookie: And I'm already sorry I said it.
> Eric: Don't be. The more you let her speak for you, the more likely you are to go on living. And you want to live, don't you? (4.2)

The central plot of the series concerns Sookie's growth from innocent to powerful woman straddling the supernatural and ordinary worlds. Seasons one and two, Sookie is mostly trying to survive as she struggles with being "vampire bait" and a tool for others to use. Season three she battles the patriarchy and Bill's vile lover Lorena on a quest to rescue her true love. It's on the quest, as she claims agency for herself, that her electrical fairy powers first emerge. In season four, she faces Marnie, destructive rage personified, who will burn every vampire, good and bad, in her quest for revenge. In five she deals with vampire Tara and her fairy kin, and six, she's drawn into the conflict between Lilith and Warlow.

There are other descents into death or near-death at the hands of René, Maryann, Bill, Russell, and others, like there are descents into dark places (the Fangtasia dungeon, the basement of the Church of the Sun, the forest, the Authority Headquarters). Each is a small death-and-rebirth sequence, offering her lessons and new inner strength. Campbell describes facing this Shadow as "destruction of the world that we have built and in which we live, and of ourselves within it; but then a wonderful reconstruction, of the bolder, cleaner, more spacious, and fully human life" (8).

This lens also offers a unique view of the other residents of Bon Temps. When analyzing characters through Jungian psychology, all appear as aspects of the self—Grandma Adele,

Arlene, Tara, Sam, Jason, and Bill all represent voices whispering inside Sookie, pushing her in different directions. By choosing which voices to embrace, Sookie grows and learns to make selfless, ethical choices.

The Heroine's Journey	Seasons 1-3	Season 4
The Call To Adventure	Bill enters the bar and falls into danger	Claudine appears to Sookie in dreams.
Refusal of the Call	Sookie hesitates	Sookie falls into a coma after Bill drains her.
The Ruthless Mentor and the Bladeless Talisman	Telepathy and mystery-solving intuition. Adele is a source of support and love.	In fairyland, Mab and Claudine are more than they appear. The light fruit they offer is deadly.
The Crossing of the First Threshold Opening One's Senses	Sookie charges outside to save Bill	Sookie battles Queen Mab, returning from fairyland far more self-assured.
Sidekicks, Trials, Adversaries	Arlene, Tara, Sam and Jason.	Pam, Tara, Jason, Holly, Jessica
Wedding the Animus Facing Bluebeard Finding the Sensitive Man Confronting the Powerless Father	She falls for Bill—both a killer and a sensitive prince. She kills the serial killer René.	Her feelings move from Bill to Eric—the helpless, clingy prince
Descent into	Battling Maryann	With Adele and

Darkness Atonement with the Mother Facing the Destroyer Integration and Apotheosis	and Lorena, she enters each of their lairs to save her loved ones.	Holly, she battles Marnie for the ones she loves.
Reward: Winning the Family	She saves Bill but is drained to the point of death and enters a coma.	On her return, she protects Eric, and saves him and Bill over and over.
Torn Desires The Magic Flight Reinstating the Family Return	Alcide and Tara drive her to safety and she struggles to reawaken.	Sookie must take a step back from her newfound power to dump both men in her life.
Power over Life and Death Ascension of the New Mother	She gains independence.	She gains magical power and wisdom.

Seasons five and six also follow this pattern as Sookie is thrust into the quest with Warlow. Though she refuses, and tries to spend all her light in a panic, Niall arrives and trains her in its use as a devastating weapon. As she deals with Warlow, learning to trick and seduce him as he's done to her, she's experiencing the Predator and Shapeshifter as prince and deciding what she will become.

The Childhood Grandmother

In the World of Common Day, as Campbell called it, the heroine lives happily at home, with no idea of the great adventure on the horizon. Adele is the perfect grandmother— always seen cooking for her family. She is entirely unmagical, and as such, she represents Sookie's safe home life. She even appears to turn a blind eye to Jason's many one-night stands and the dark side of Bill's vampire nature.

However, she's not ignorant or in denial like many fantasy parents, from Harry Potter's aunt and uncle to Buffy's mother. Though she doesn't appear to discuss it much, she's aware that her husband "knew about people." When Jason is suspected of the season one murders, Adele urges Sookie to use her mind reading and discover the real killer. It seems a proper lady is allowed to use her gifts, even ones they don't discuss, to save her family from harm.

It's a well-known trope that the good parents or mentors always die in the hero quest. Sookie's parents are already dead, and her grandmother dies in season one. Eric's maker, the saintly Godric, dies in season two, and Bill's Lorena (admittedly a more complicated maternal-sexual relationship) dies in season three. Sookie's fairy godmother and Sam and Tommy's parents die in season four. Evil mentor figures Maryann and Marnie perish as well.

Sheldon Cashdan explains in the fairytale study *The Witch Must Die*:

> The mother's exit, paradoxically, is empowering in that it forces the children in the story to confront a cruel and

dangerous world on their own. Lacking a mother or
protector, the hero or heroine must draw on inner resources
that might not have been tested were the mother still
around. (42)

To grow, characters must leave behind the source of protection
and care. Clarissa Pinkola Estés, author of the psychological
fairytale study *Women Who Run with the Wolves,* adds that a
woman's psychic chores include the following:

Accepting that the ever-watchful, hovering, protective,
psychic mother is not adequate as a central guide for one's
future instinctual life (the too-good mother dies). Taking on
the task of being on one's own, developing one's own
consciousness about danger, intrigue, politics. Becoming
alert by oneself, for oneself. (81)

However, the mentors' influences live on, as Eric dreams of
Godric and Sookie repeats her grandmother's sayings and keeps
her values alive. After she dies, her home remains a major
character in the story. In season four, Sookie asks Marnie for a
reading and her grandmother sends her a message, warning her
against falling in love with Eric and being near Marnie. Unlike
the traditional scene in which the medium is the only channel,
Sookie actually hears her grandmother's thoughts, warning her
of danger. At season end, Adele appears in person to offer
Sookie more advice, that there's nothing to fear in being alone.
When Sookie hears this, she understands that it's all right to
leave Eric and Bill behind and discover who she is without the
warring vampires. Season five, Adele's spirit provides another
crucial piece of information—that the family's dealings with
Warlow are under Sookie's bed. Even after her death, Adele
remains a link with the past and wise guide for the future.

Defender of the Helpless

> Bill is captured by two drainers and it is Sookie who rescues him, taking them on alone, overpowering the male drainer by attacking him with a chain and threatening the female drainer with his knife. From this first encounter, Sookie is established as a brave and fearless active heroine. (Brick 53)

On her classic journey, the heroine quests to protect the weak: saving children, little siblings, and lovers is a metaphor for creating a family for herself and becoming their defender, then finally, guardian of the community.

> Her goal is to become the all-powerful mother. Thus, many heroines set out on missions to rescue their shattered families: Meg Murray of *A Wrinkle in Time* quests to save her father then her little brother. Coraline tries to save her parents, Meggie of *Inkheart* and Clary of *The Mortal Instruments,* their mothers. Tim Burton's Alice tries to rescue the Mad Hatter. Scores of young women in folklore rescue their lovers from fairies, demons, and ogres. Demeter forces herself into the realm of the dead to reclaim her daughter, while Isis scours the world for her husband's broken body. Katniss, of course, spends the series protecting Prim and her growing adoptive family, from Peeta to the children of Panem. (Frankel, *Many Faces of Katniss* 113-114)

Sookie's magical gift is mind-reading, but also a particular kind of perception. "It was one of those nights that made me wonder how the humans around me could be so oblivious to the other world operating right beside ours. Only willful ignorance could ignore the charge of magic in the air," she notes (*Dead as a Doornail* 11). Anna Paquin notes that her own extrasensory ability is "Good old-fashioned female intuition. That's about it…I don't think I'd be out of line in saying it's just part of the way women interact with the world" (Martin). In fact, vampires' approaches are sped up on the show, while time often slows during Sookie's telepathic moments, emphasizing her attention to everything around her. Telepathy is a bigger liability for the heroine—Harris deliberately designed Sookie's telepathy as a disability, "something that would draw [her and Bill] to one another, united in being outsiders from mainstream society" (Wilcott 26).

In *Dead and Gone,* Sookie realizes that she sees her role as a barmaid as nurturing, fussing over those around her. In the books, she eventually becomes a co-owner of Merlotte's, turning this nurturing into a stable business for herself. Her hospitality in her own home is likewise a vital part of her nurturing Southern identity and upbringing. One interview with author Charlaine Harris notes:

> Over the years, the kick-ass heroine has always had a hot dish for anyone in need, and always a Coke or a True Blood in the fridge, for humans and supes alike. This, it turns out, is just what you do in the south where Harris grew up, "The first thing you do in the south is ask visitors what they'd like to drink and then if they're anywhere around mealtime you ask if they wanna eat with you. In the south I grew up in, that was the norm." (Tyley, "Charlaine Harris on Death Threats")

Her contrasting quest in each book is that of telepathic detective. This is a quest of perception, emphasized by Sookie's extra-sensory telepathy. "The detective story and the gothic romance emphasize the female hero's role as a sleuth, who discovers the truth behind deceptive appearances" (Pearson and Pope 69).

On the show, Sookie's entering the witches' lair stops the vampires from killing everyone in it, most of whom are unwilling hostages. In the corresponding fourth book, Sookie personally yanks the innocents from combat. When Sookie works as a lie detector for Eric Northman, she insists a condition be that the culprit be turned over to the authorities unharmed. She finally risks her life in the Church of the Sun to rescue Godric. Her concern is always for the innocents around her, even those she doesn't know personally. It's not surprising Warlow disguises himself as a wounded half-fae, knowing all she'll do to protect him.

She charges into Maryann's lair and Lorena's as well to save her friends—Sookie first uses her electrical energy defending Sam from Maryann and offers her life for a dying Bill. She's the one to hide an amnesiac Eric and comfort Jason over and over. When she does know the person, she offers all she has, as in the case of the fatally-wounded Tara. Seeing her friend cannot survive, Sookie is the one to summon Pam and promise her anything in the world to save her.

In one of the later books, Sookie volunteers her telepathy to the local police then the rescue workers when a vampire summit turns deadly. Even her fear of exposure is nothing compared with saving lives. However, while she feels guilty for not saving lives on a permanent basis, she decides it isn't worth sacrificing the life she enjoys. The final two books see her saving a life in dramatic fashion, as she chooses the romantic partner she truly loves and wants to commit her life to.

Sookie Enters the Gothic Narrative
Sookie is very much a daylight girl, with her blonde ponytail and pastels. She says, "I'm a summer person. I like the sun and the short dresses, and the feeling you had many hours of light to do whatever you chose" (*Club Dead* 34). Sam (who often transforms into a dog) dresses Sookie as a bunny for Halloween, the ultimate bait for every kind of predator. "Your blood tastes like freedom, Sookie. Like sunshine in a pretty blonde bottle," Eric tells her (4.2). This is the irresistible draw for vampires—the side of themselves they've had to do without. Perpetually sunbathing and wearing shorts, golden-haired Sookie is a daylight child (in the books Niall tells her she's so drawn to the sun because of her fairy blood).

Eric cuddles up to Sookie to listen to her heartbeat and pretend his own is beating. Both he and Bill hang around Sookie while she's eating and engaging in her human life—though they're condemned to the darkness, they want a taste of light.

When the vampire Bill enters her world, the bar, she's exposed to the supernatural world of darkness and horror, all she's isn't. She is the classic innocent maid drawn into a gothic adventure, the crossing of the threshold into unnatural or magical space where the normal rules don't apply. As soon as Bill walks into her bar, Sookie's story changes from humdrum to magical. Nothing will ever be the same. She descends further into the Otherworld whenever she goes to visit him. "The graveyard and the Compton house constitute the most traditionally gothic settings in Bon Temps" (Ruddell and Cherry 46). To reach Bill, Sookie must pass through both, "figuratively passing from day to night and from life to death as she goes to her liaisons with him" (Ruddell and Cherry 46).

This monstrous otherness is compelling as well as frightening. It's also a path to deeper mystical knowledge for the heroine. When Sookie drinks from Bill, she sees "visions all with a background of darkness," visions of hunting in the woods, chasing prey and smelling its blood (*Dead Until Dark* 197). After both her third drink of vampire blood and her third drink of Eric's blood specifically, book Sookie wonders if she's transforming into a vampire. While in fact she isn't, she's growing to understand their way of life in the magical world as she shares their fear and happiness through the blood bond.

At the same time, the supernatural world is where she's the Chosen One, where she has gifts rather than a curse. In *From Dead to Worse,* Sam asks if Sookie had been happier before the vampires came to town. Sookie says she wasn't, telling him, "Every day was a struggle just to act like I was a regular human, like I didn't know all the things I know about other humans…Knowing about the supernatural world puts all that in a different perspective…Plus, it's nice to be valued for the very thing that makes regular people think I'm just a crazy girl" (271).

In the first episode, she's awed by the mysterious Vampire Bill and embarrassed by the dirty talk among the other waitresses. However, the second season sees her marketing her telepathy to Eric, treating it as a useful service, not a secret disability. After drinking Bill's blood, Sookie feels stronger, braver, more confident, and "more secure in my sexuality and its power," as she puts it (*Dead Until Dark* 210). By season three, she's running the show as all the supernatural creatures crave her, from Alcide and Sam to the vampires.

"Like all gothic texts, *True Blood* is obsessively concerned with questions relating to bodily boundaries and their transgression" (Waters 35). Bodies on *True Blood* are especially vulnerable, emphasized through both penetrated bodies and spaces and other types of boundary crossing. Sookie's mind is constantly assailed by others' voices, to the point where she feels she can never date another human.

The house is symbol for Sookie, sometimes stable and secure, sometimes invaded by vampires. Sookie's house is terribly fragile, as her own psyche is as she resists being devoured. In the first season, she finds her grandmother dead on the floor, and in the kitchen, she discovers her friend René is the murderer. The season one murders take place in women's houses, often the bedrooms, in what is meant to be a private sanctuary. "The architectural borders of Sookie's home are subject to perpetual breach: vampires, werewolves, shapeshifters, maenads, and a serial killer all find their way past the Stackhouse threshold, shattering the illusion that the home is—or ever can be—immune to the threats of the outside world" (Waters 35). When Maryann has taken it over, Sookie charges in to protect her gran's house from its terrible defilement. In season three, werewolves attack repeatedly, and Debbie makes Sookie a murderer, invading her ethical security at the same time as her walls. It's still Sookie's refuge from the magical world, as a word from her sends the vampires flying out her door.

And, in a post-modern twist, the show contains many references to television, which some critics describe as the ultimate invasion into the American home, with its chatter and commercials. "Offering frequent depictions of audio-visual equipment, *True Blood* is forever commenting on its own status as a television show, and thus on its own 'dangerous' potential to deceive or mislead the viewer" (Waters 36). Maudette Pickens pretends to be strangled on a video to psyche out Jason…and fools us as well. Jason dances in underwear to titillate viewers, on a show that's full of nudity to titillate viewers. Nan Flanagan's broadcasts as she debates vampire policy satirize and highlight the media and current events in our own society.

Gothic is concerned with excess—as such the over and

beyond sex, violence, and profanity on the series set it apart. Likewise, "the show's gory explosions of tissue and matter would seem to materialize the logic of the gothic in ways that other vampire fiction cannot" (Waters 35). What should traditionally be hidden (like the vampires' insides and grisly deaths), is hideously brought to light "in a spectacle of compelling sanguinary splendor" (Waters 35). Exposure of secrets and the hidden is a key gothic component.

In Bon Temps, characters lead double lives, from Miss Jeanette's prosaic drugstore job to René the murderer and Sam the shifter. Even the humans of Bon Temps are monstrous. "Characters such as Maxine Fortenberry, Andy Bellefleur, René Lenier, Joe Lee Mickens, Lettie Mae Thornton, and the Newlins are all signified as grotesque in various ways and provide depth to the narrative" (Ruddell and Cherry 40). We see murder, child abuse, infidelity, drug abuse, and more, all in this small town that's as riddled with darkness under its pleasant façade as *Desperate Housewives*. Located as it is in the old-fashioned, rural, deep South, Bon Temps is an "ideal location for barely-concealed prejudices, buried secrets, and damaged relationships" (Ruddell and Cherry 49).

Pam and Nan Flanagan emphasize the surface versus hidden world in their dress. On television, Nan wears professional suits, but she dresses as a more classic vampire when "off duty." Pam by contrast, wears a black leather corset and gauntlets on duty at Fangtasia, but on her own prefers pink suits, pencil skirts, or twinsets with pearls and pumps. Her vampire costumes are performance, subverted by her more upscale reality. Fangtasia looks like vampire Disneyland with neon logos, posters, and kitsch souvenirs. Below, however, is a real dungeon where Lafayette nearly dies.

Sookie wears a classic white nightgown for her first tryst with Bill, but she's embracing the darkness, not hiding from it like traditional virgin heroines. Similarly Willa in season six wears a white nightgown for the full-on vampire seduction scene as Eric raps at her window, carries her off, and finally turns her. However, she too, is eager to enter the darkness. Both times, it is the men who are reticent to form such a serious attachment. Franklin dresses Tara in a similar nightgown, but their encounter is likewise subverted, as "Tara is anything but submissive or cowed by Franklin" (Ruddell and Cherry 49). Gothic is a tale of the innocent heroine and the terrifying monster and can also be seen as a metaphor for romance with the frightening and mysterious Other. In traditional gothic romance, "the female protagonist's character evolves and grows in a kind of dance with the journeys that the gothic heroes take, alternatively gravitating towards them and fleeing to elude them" (Mukherjea 119). In the DVD commentary on the show's first episode, Alan Ball said the series is about "the terrors of intimacy," a concept emphasized by the monsters-as-lovers.

In his seminal theoretical work on horror, *The Philosophy of Horror*, Noël Carroll defines monsters in literary horror as inexplicable by our current scientific knowledge, a disturbing mixture of different elements that defies classification (40). They cross the boundaries between living and dead, or (in the case of werewolves and shifters) human and animal. Monsters "are unnatural relative to a culture's conceptual scheme of nature. They don't fit the scheme; they violate it" (34). This very unnaturalness creates fear and horror in the reader or viewer.

Certainly Bill and Eric are alluring, but when Bill twists Lorena's head half-off and they continue enjoying rough sex, or when he bursts from the ground where he's been functionally dead to seduce Sookie, there's a sense of visceral revulsion. They are undead corpses, lacking pulses, warmth, or a need to breathe. Yet they walk among us.

Caroll adds that monsters are "not only quite dangerous but they also make one's skin creep" (23). Threats to the body and the self are a common horror trope, seen on *True Blood* as the were-panthers not only rape Jason but try to transform him, or vampires bite and then drink their prey to death. Too much blood-drinking could mean being turned into an undead creature, forced to maintain a nocturnal, even subhuman existence. As Sookie allows the vampires to feed on her, this is a constant source of worry, as well as enticement.

This is modern gothic, subverted with technology and a touch of science fiction weaponry as well as its contemporary issues and reimagining of the tropes. "Bill and Eric are grotesque in their undead and sometimes amoral vampire nature but highly structured and distinct in their manner of *living*" (Mukherjea 114). Eric runs his bar as a strong corporation, and Bill is busy hiring contractors to modernize his house. As monsters existing in the real world, they likewise subvert their roles with a polite face of American businessmen and property owners. As such they bridge the gap between the worlds and become contenders for the position of romantic hero.

The Unconscious World
Sookie's pleasant white cottage is like a beacon, surrounded by fairytale woods. A short drive away is Fangtasia, the nocturnal Otherworld in a sense. This is the territory of vampires, and Bill hesitates to bring Sookie there. In a white dress spotted with little red flowers like bloodstains she looks "like vampire bait" —an innocent ready to be devoured.

> Compared to the rural Bon Temps, Fangtasia is Big City, Sexy Shreveport, and everything that implies to a person from a small town. It's lights, flash, glamor, temptation, and things that go bump in the night. It's attractive, yet dangerous—something that perhaps draws a person out for a night or two. But it's not Bon Temps, not home. (Lima 36).

As Christopher Vogler reflects in his book on the hero's journey, "A Special World, even a figurative one, has a different feel, a different rhythm, different priorities and values, and different rules" (136). In Fangtasia, Bill watches over Sookie, since her life is literally on the line. Eric can murder his employees (though only in private, he insists) or seduce them in the basement. In his feudal kingdom, he cares nothing for drained and glamoured humans or the police, only visits from the Magister. Modern America seems to stop at the door.

> Sookie: I'm not some kind of prisoner you can just lock up any time you feel like taking off.
> Eric: Actually, you are.
> Sookie: Let me go ! I knew I shouldn't have trusted you.
> Eric: You were right. (3.10)

The other bar is Merlotte's. It's the normal bar (as much as one can have such a thing) and Sookie's home base. In fact, Sookie continues to consider Merlotte's a "home," no matter how many unsavory creatures invade it. Sookie works there in innocent green and white, perky ponytail bobbing as she brings people plates of homestyle cooking.

Fangtasia is its shadow, the unreal, touristy bar where normal can encounter frightening vampires, get chained up against their wills, and nearly die. Actually, as much of that happens at Merlotte's as at Fangtasia. By season three, the dead waitresses have become a running joke or at least a cautionary tale. Corpses and vampires appear in the walk-in fridge. Maenad devotees capture Sam there and were-panthers attack the bar.

As Sookie works at Merlotte's, she meets any number of characters—it's a place of neutral territory where the nastiest racists mix with the most committed of vampires. Sookie meets Bill at Merlotte's, Jessica meets Hoyt, and Tara meets Franklin. TruBlood and Lafayette's "burger with the AIDS" are served alongside classic comfort food and plenty of alcohol.

Christopher Vogler, describing the hero's journey, adds:

> The Watering Hole is a natural congregating place and a good spot to observe and get information...The crossing of the First Threshold may have been long, lonely and dry. Bars are natural spots to recuperate, pick up gossip, make friends, and confront enemies. They allow us to observe people under pressure, when true character is revealed. (140)

Significant bars as gathering places appear in *Star Wars, Shane, Casablanca,* and *Buffy the Vampire Slayer,* all stories of two worlds mixing. Maria Lima adds in her *True Blood* essay, "Home Is Where the Bar Is":

> Every TV show has one: that place that when you go there, you're part of the club, one of the gang, an insider—a home away from house, a place where you feel comfortable, whether diner, bar, or pool hall. Cheers, the popular 1990s comedy, revolved around a Boston bar, while Friends

> characters hung out at Central Perk, a coffee house. On Star Trek: Deep Space Nine, you'd often find the officers, residents, and visiting aliens at Quark's, and on Star Trek: The Next Generation, the place to be was Ten Forward. (Lima 33-34)

It's also a microcosm of their world and their lives—folks gather there to whisper uneasily about the murders or bring their prejudices and conflicts into the concentrated hotbed of the single room. Arlene's hatred for vampires like Jessica, Hoyt's love triangle, Sam's awkward relationship with his brother all are exacerbated by the small space.

"Merlotte's reflects and encapsulates the emotional arc of the show. In season one, it's all about getting to know the people, the situations, and where folks fit in. In season two, the happenings at the bar reflect the breaking down of those established roles and expectations" (Lima 34-35). The maenad's influence is the most dramatic version of this, as a dance party breaks out to Sam's dismay (banning dancing and religion appear to be his only two rules). Later the clientele turn savage and wage war on Sam, determined to capture and sacrifice him. Chaos has broken out, and no one is safe.

Hot Wings, the fairy strip club, is the anti-vampire sanctuary, but in accomplishing its goals, it becomes incredibly similar to Fangtasia. Both parody their own culture, from Pam's black corsets to Hadley's Halloween store fairy wings. Both cater to human tourists who want to walk on the wild side. The fairy club is also like the shadow of the fairies' tranquil paradise: amidst loud music and hot pink, everyone entertains humans rather than harvesting them. At the same time, it's a place of power and hidden truths: Hadley dresses as a fairy, revealing her nature to the world. And the fairies offer Sookie the truth about her parents' death.

The hero's or heroine's journey is all about facing one's Shadow, the repressed nature that's been buried and rejected from the conscious self—the rage, hatred, fear and other primitive emotions. Some Jungians maintain that the Shadow "contains, besides the personal shadow, the shadow of society [...] fed by the neglected and repressed collective values"

(Fordham 5). As Campbell notes:

> The unconscious sends all sorts of vapors, odd beings, terrors and deluding images up into the mind—whether in dream, broad daylight, or insanity; for the human kingdom, beneath the floor of the comparatively neat little dwelling that we call our consciousness, goes down into unexpected Aladdin caves. There not only jewels but also dangerous jinn abide: the inconvenient or resisted psychological powers that we have not thought or dared to integrate into our lives. (8)

The were-infested woods, the dark Authority with its cells beneath—these are manifestations of the unconscious world. Bon Temps, pleasant and happy as it seems (in fact, the name means "good times") is filled with darkness under a thin veneer of civilization. Hidden beneath the surface is child abuse, hidden powers, family secrets, in "the isolating and constraining nature of one's over-small, over-tight community" (Mukherjea 119).

> The town's corruption remained hidden, underground—nothing in plain sight. Jason and newcomer Amy's abduction of the vampire Eddie took place in Jason's basement; Lettie Mae and Tara's exorcisms with the "psychic" Miss Jeannette happened deep in the woods; even the most important moments in Sookie's relationship with Bill happened mostly elsewhere (he courted her at her home, bedded her at his). (Lima 40)

Old European fantasy is set in ancient crumbling castles or the dark forest. In the developed modern US, rural small-town Louisiana works as a setting in its own way—what if Miss Jeannette's voodoo or Jesus' brujo training really work? The insular, inbred family of Hotshot have reason to keep secrets and distrust strangers—they're actually inbred were-panthers. In a world where ancestry and old-world aristocracy is everything, wouldn't be a thrill to meet one's Civil War-fighting ancestors in the (undead) flesh? And racism likewise is modernized as vampires Bill and Jessica find a burning cross on their lawn.

The forest is private in a different way, dark and primal.

> The forest, a feminine symbol, represents the dangerous
> side of the unconscious, its ability to destroy reason. As
> foliage blocks the masculine-centered sun's rays, it
> becomes a hidden place, a place of unknown perils and
> obscurity. This setting forth reflects the adolescent's inner
> turmoil, as the unconscious intrudes into the everyday
> world. Since innovative psychologists like Freud and Jung
> represented myths as part of the masculine cultural
> unconscious, femininity was constructed as the
> unconscious of the unconscious, the dark continent of the
> dark continent. (Frankel, *Girl to Goddess* 59)

Shifters like Sam, Daphne, and Crystal are all found in the woods experiencing their animal selves. It's where Eric and Sookie and also Jason and Crystal begin their relationships. It's also the location of the Rattrays' attacks on Bill and Sookie and the place where René attempts to murder Sookie. Maryann attacks Sookie there and Marnie curses Pam with the decay spell. To Sookie, the forest is a place of sweltering heat and pressure as mysterious monsters wait to devour her: "Sweat poured down my face and my hair was sticking to my neck. A devil's walking stick scratched me deeply enough to make me bleed" (*Deadlocked* 163).

All this transition between the night and day worlds begins to cast the night world as the "normal" one as Sookie spends more time there and discovers her fairy nature. By contrast the sunny, daytime world is a fragile frontage, concealing the dangers of racism and abuse beneath its pleasant surface. Sookie ditches her job every season to go on rescue missions for the vampires—life and death supersedes table-waiting. Her normal life matters to her, as her family defines her life. However, a vampire hater murders her grandmother, and were-panthers capture Jason—the dark world breaks into her light world as surely as werewolves and maenads lay waste to her house each season.

Sookie's Animus Growth
The Animus is the masculine force in the heroine's life, her inner voice and the best friends and lovers who echo that voice.

It "connects the woman with her spiritual side, making her even more receptive to her own creativity" (Frankel, *Girl to Goddess* 23). In quest stories, this is the male sidekick, like Dorothy's friends in Oz who not-so-subtly represent brains, heart, and courage. With those allies beside her, the heroine learns about traits outside herself and trains for the ultimate confrontations.

Sookie grows up with Jason, the overgrown child who's all impulse and emotional neediness. "As far as intimacy and companionship goes, I had to admit that he hardly counted," Sookie notes (*Club Dead* 10). His ill-considered actions and passion for women get him thrown in jail for murder in the first season. Alan Ball describes Jason as a "somewhat dimwitted, emotionally stunted, sexually compulsive jock." By the second season, he's become more of a force for useful plans, though his rash shooting of Eggs devastates him.

The Animus

The Animus Growth Within the Heroine	Trait	Positive Aspect	Negative Aspect
1. Passion and Physical Force	Emotion	Mutual devotion	Mutual rage and destruction
2. Initiative and Planning	Body	Useful plans and action	Harmful, ill-considered acts
3. Law, Rule, and Order	Mind	Self-restraint and moral advice	Inflexible obstruction
4. Wisdom and Spiritual Fulfillment	Spirit	Guide to self-knowledge and ascension	Deceiver and distorter of the future

Lafayette, too, is a creature of body and impulse. His dealings with the vampires all blow up in his face, leaving him fearing for his life from Eric and Pam. When desperate, he offers them his body and his skills, acknowledging that that's where his power can be found: "I'm already a person of poor moral character. So, I hit the ground running and I damn near glamour people already. Gimme what ya'll got. Not only will I be a badass vampire, but I'd be your badass vampire" (2.2). Only in training with brujo and romantic interest Jesus Velasquez does Lafayette begin to expand his mind. Gaining more power, whether with drugs or magic, ends tragically for him as he loses his freedom then Jesus and is subject to possession several times. However, though he grows in experience, he doesn't significantly change his behavior.

Eric can be described similarly—he's all a creature of impulse, who alternates between useful plans and insights and the ill-considered murders that doom them all. Allied with him, Sookie trains in emotion and knowledge of the body, even as she strives for higher wisdom. She learns to subvert authority, often in the person of Eric the sheriff as she bargains for money and favors.

Bill, meanwhile, is a force of the mind—all of his acts are controlled and carefully considered. However, his inflexibility can hinder him as he refuses to compromise when raising Jessica or negotiating with other vampires. In season four, he takes on much more responsibility as King of Louisiana. In his paternal mansion, with security guards and jail cells, he controls all the vampires of Bon Temps. He controls humans as well, manipulating them with glamour, press conferences, and ribbon cuttings alongside the mayor. With his new authority, he evolves a better relationship with Jessica, and they becomes a more solid father-daughter pair. He's also a stronger part of the vampire hierarchy, as he pledges loyalty to the Authority. As Sookie finds herself contending with vampire laws and the vampire hierarchy, Bill is an invaluable guide.

Sam looks out for Sookie. "I can take a lot of paternalism, but I was about up to my ears" she relates when Sam insists on discussing her trip to Mississippi with Alcide (*Club Dead* 64). Nonetheless, he protects her like an older brother, though he comes to look out for Tara as well—In season one, Sam gives Tara the money for an exorcism and promises Bill he'll watch over Sookie. He runs Merlotte's like a family, and Sookie is his responsibility. As she acknowledges multiple times in the books, Sam makes sure no one molests his female employees or insults them. He quietly acknowledges Sookie's mind reading power and welcomes her into his head as the ultimate safe place. Nearly uniquely, he doesn't mind her powers like the townsfolk or seek to use them for his own gain as the vampires repeatedly do. His bar remains a sanctuary through the series, with Sam as landlord, protector, and advisor and taker-in of lost strays. His advice is often of the mind—he's a thinker and planner, though he occasionally gives in to rage.

Not until the later seasons, when Niall shows up to mentor Sookie, does she find a true wise guide. He tells her truths about her life with the fairies and vampires and provides her with training in using her gifts. Even after he leaves, she continues training, determined to beat the crafty Warlow, the ultimate deceiver.

The Prince

Sara Buttsworth in "Cinderbella: Twilight, Fairy Tales, and the Twenty-First Century American Dream" notes, "'Forget Princess, I want to be a Vampire' sums up an entire culture whose ideal of having it all conflicts with the realities of income differences and sexual inequality that still characterize American society" (67). In *Twilight*, for instance, Edward is the devastatingly handsome, wealthy, and enticing vampire. At last, he transforms his human love Bella. She can now be with the Cullens forever, perpetually healthy and rich with a new family to protect her.

> Being swept off, every decision made, with no way to return is the perfect fantasy. There can be no turning back or divorce for Bella the vampire. She can spend eternity with her Edward, cared for by a host of vampire relatives and seemingly endless funds. No hard choices need present themselves ever again, and in a true fairytale style, Bella can not only live happily ever after but remain eternally beautiful. (Frankel, *Many Faces of Katniss* 63)

Though Sookie isn't interested in being turned, she's quickly absorbed into Bill's world of vampire privilege. Her actress, Anna Paquin, notes, "They're sexy and dangerous and always really hot. And they've been around a long time-they probably know what they're doing" (Martin). Bill of course is the prince of the tale with his old-fashioned Southern charm. He arranges a bodyguard for Sookie when she's in danger, an act the other waitresses call "romantic" (*Dead Until Dark* 241). And as he points out, he isn't used to modern ways, so Sookie can excuse his pushy, old-fashioned treatment of her.

Bill doesn't just induct her into sex, he brushes her hair, carries her and bathes her. "Every now and then I felt like I was Bill's doll," she relates (*Dead Until Dark* 192). Bill calls Sookie a child and early in season two insists constantly (like in Sookie's dealings with Eric and Jessica) that he knows best. Later, he perfectly scripts out his proposal to Sookie, renting the entire French restaurant and sending her a lavender gown. Alan Ball reveals that this was designed to give the couple a "moment of happiness, a hope that something they thought was off-limits to both of them was actually within their grasp" (qtd. in *The Sookie Stackhouse Companion* 282).

In the third book, when Bill chooses Lorena over Sookie, he intends to arrange Sookie's "future care"—give her money when he breaks up with her (*Club Dead* 47). When Sookie feels financially strapped, she reminds herself that Bill will be happy to solve all those problems for her (*Club Dead* 76). Jungian analyst Connie Zweig notes that this is a common pattern: "Women with absent fathers may project their imagined, perfect ideals onto men, forever searching for 'the one that got away,' who has the power to make all things right" (186). Bill can be her source of finances, protection, and thrills, as well as romance. Thus, Sookie gravitates to powerful, mysterious wealthy vampires Eric and Bill over the more down-to-earth Sam and Alcide.

Of course, allowing the magical problem solver to take care of everything is infantilizing, treating the boyfriend as father and protector instead of equal. In the *Twilight* series, Bella has similar moments in her relationship with Edward the incredibly wealthy vampire: when prom comes around, Edward brings over a gown along with his sister to do Bella's hair and makeup. For her birthday, the vampires buy and install a stereo for her truck, and Edward later buys her a bulletproof car. Her honeymoon is arranged from travel arrangements to packing to secret destination, and she returns home to find a new fairytale cottage, furniture, and a closet of clothes in her size. She has become the entitled princess.

Indeed, princess culture is stronger than ever recently, despite nineties girl power. Alongside dystopias and action-adventures comes the image of the wealthy, high handed prince stridently announcing "She is mine!" (as Bill says quite often) and the common-born, blue collar girl who secretly loves it. The girl does not become active or accomplish goals, but instead waits for a prince to complete her. This especially appears in teen fairytale adaptations like *Tiger's Curse* and *The Selection,* while *Twilight* is very much a retelling of Beauty and the Beast. Katniss is forced into her princess gowns and remains ambiguous about them, but she's still caught in a story of the princely mentor who garbs her like a princess.

After Bill "arranges" things for Sookie, including the murder of her "funny uncle," Sookie cringes. She begins to find it creepy, noting, "It's like dating the Godfather, Bill. I'm scared to say anything around you now" (*Dead Until Dark* 166). However, she also welcomes his protection—his heavy-handed demand that "she is mine" protects her from the other vampires. When he insists she goes to see Eric, she thinks, "I had to stop myself from begging, please don't let the bad vampire hurt me. Please don't let the bad vampire rape me" (*Dead Until Dark* 194).

> She wants a happy fantasy life with Bill; her man completes her. She lives out her small-town values with little conflict, despite being a cultural outsider and now a "fangbanger." (The sex scenes between Bill and Sookie are also a bit more romance novel cover than they are empowered egalitarian pleasure exchanges, blood aside.) Sookie's also not much on traditional feminist independence. She lived with her grandmother well into her twenties. (Mamatas 65)

Of course, Eric is a prince as well, repainting Sookie's house and buying her a flatscreen TV, and even commissioning a lightproof closet for himself. On her return from fairyland, Sookie is just dropping her slumpie blue robe for a hot pink nightie when Eric invades her bedroom. As she clutches the inadequate covering over herself alluringly, Eric tells her that the house, and thus her bedroom and everything in it, are his.

> Sookie: Why would you do that? Why would you buy my house?
> Eric: Because I always knew you were alive, and if I owned the house, then I would own you. Sookie, you are mine. (4.1)

As he uses the words Bill once used, their romance begins in earnest. Eric's instincts were true—buying Sookie's house has bought him Sookie. Though she yells at Eric for buying her house, he doesn't pursue her plans to take legal action once she discovers he's the owner. In her acknowledgement that's she's keeping the flatscreen, there's a tacit acceptance of his interference in her life.

Facing Death

Sookie has many brushes with death in the first season. She meets Bill when the Rattrays nearly kill him, then try to kill her in the following episode. Many other corpses follow. Of course her greatest experience of death in her grandmother's passing. There's also her great-uncle's death, which alerts Sookie to Bill's violent nature. She has three brushes with death herself, from the savage Rattrays seeking retaliation, to Eric's thieving employee trying to kill her, to her final battle with Rene.

The murder mystery is an important step in Sookie's growth. Understanding Rene, reading his savage mind and saving herself and her community from him transform her. No longer meek little Sookie, she becomes a killer and psychic detective. Further, she faces one of the darkest forces that can be found in the mind. The Predator is a part of the self, the dark Animus that knows exactly which words will most devastate.

The predator exists in everyone—the force that longs to devour the world, the insatiable greed that will take the entire psyche for itself. The demon lover, or killer animus, lures his victim out of life. He seduces her, shrouding her in lies, trying to convince her she's helpless. (Frankel, *Girl to Goddess* 82)

"Her Animus assures her that she is lonely and nobody and nothing and will never get anywhere—the sadist within tells her that," Von Franz explains (*The Feminine in Fairy Tales* 71). René thinks of her as a fangbanger, a lover of monstrous undead creatures, and Sookie must face that truth in herself and learn to accept it.

René begins by killing the waitresses, Sookie's symbolic sisters at Merlotte's. Then René kills Sookie's gran, and shortly after Bill is apparently murdered. As the deaths continue, Jason is locked up, possibly forever. As the Predator tears apart the heroine's psyche, he's devoted to "the killing of the creative feminine, the one who has the potential to develop all manner of new and interesting aspects" (Estés 56-57). He's a killer of women, the creative, loving enablers like Amy and Gran.

Sam, the safe male, rushes to save her in the forest, as Andy and Jason slowly learn Sookie was right about the murderer's identity. Last but most importantly, Bill sacrifices himself to walk into daylight and try to save Sookie. The masculine forces in Sookie's life are gathering to support her. However, significantly, she rescues herself. A corner has been turned, and the world will never be the same.

Sookie's Allies as Shadows
Sookie has many reflections—the friends who are what she could have been if she'd chosen another path—Arlene has multiple husbands and children, Hadley is a vampire's victim, Pam is Eric's "other half" after she begs him to turn her into a creature of the night. As such, they all reflect Sookie's might-have-beens, cautionary tales, and options as she decides her future. When she meets each of them, she understands herself and her own life-choices better.

Arlene

Unlike Tara's closed-off suspicion, Arlene maintains "incredible optimism about men, even after four marriages" (*Club Dead* 157). She's an earth mother, always worried about her children and her long term relationships. "She had a great zest for life, she had an easy chemistry with men, she had 2 cute children, and she made her own living. These were enviable things to lonely me," Sookie notes (*Dead Ever After* 72). Arlene's husbands are all human, and she can have a job, a home, and children. She and Terry have a happy give-and take as they work side-by-side in Merlotte's, a life Sookie could have if she chose Sam. Arlene also loathes vampires and cautions Sookie to protect herself from them. Sookie, chatting with her friend and babysitting her children, is tempted to follow this path, even as she continues to date and work in the supernatural world.

Hadley

Hadley, Sookie's cousin, is completely in thrall to the vampire queen, as Sookie later chooses not to be to Bill the vampire king. Hadley is a pawn like Sookie is, as Eric and the queen play chicken with her life. Further, Eric drinks from her and gives her blood, as he longs to do with Sookie herself.

In the books, Hadley was a popular girl, cheerleader, and even Miss Teen Bon Temps, compared with outcast Sookie. She's also transformed into a vampire, who is murdered and leaves Sookie to crack the case and complete her last mission ("One-Word Answer" 91-96). As Sookie tries on Hadley's clothes and sleeps in her bed, she reflects on committing completely to a vampire and the consequences of that lifestyle. Hadley also had a telepathic son, forcing Sookie to reflect on the consequences to her future children, if they inherit the gift.

Barry the Bellboy

Though it's unusual for the shadow or foil to be the opposite gender from the protagonist, Barry is another possible outcome of Sookie's life. Miserable from his telepathy, he hides from fellow telepath Sookie just as she attempts to reach out.

Barry: Why won't you leave me alone?
Sookie: Because I've never met another telepath. Have you?
Barry: No, and don't say that word.
Sookie: It's what you are. Nobody else knows what it's like to be us. We need to stick together. It's nothing to be ashamed of. (2.5)

As she says this to her friend, she says it to herself as well and slowly comes to believe it. Barry, however, doesn't.

Barry: Yes it is! My life is shit. I can't do anything normal people do. If I'm not around a bunch of vampires, I can't hardly think straight.
Sookie: I used to feel exactly the same. Like I had a disability.
Barry: More like a curse.
Sookie: But lately since I met my boyfriend, it seems like telepathy can come in handy some times. You can even make a little money.
Barry: Then you're even crazier than I am. (2.5)

His warning proves prophetic, as the vampires exploit her and endanger her more than they pay her for her trouble. As such, he's a warning voice inside her, one she fails to heed in time. He's eventually captured by the fairies, and likely doesn't escape, another fate that easily could be Sookie's.

Hugo
Hugo, boyfriend to Isabel the vampire, is another cautionary tale for Sookie. He confronts her with the questions she's refused to ask herself, wondering if she wants to be turned before she ages and Bill grows tired of her. However, his own lover's refusal to turn him drives him into despair, and he betrays all the vampires. Like Barry, he voices the deepest thoughts of Sookie's conscience:

Hugo: It's addictive, isn't it? To be desired by something that powerful.
Sookie: I'm not addicted.
Hugo: No. I guess you wouldn't know how your life changes

to suit them. You start missing work, can't get up in the
morning, can't stand to leave them after dark. Before you
know, you're somebody you don't even recognize.
Sookie: So you went to the Fellowship 'cause you can't
control yourself?
Hugo: I begged her to turn me. It's the only way we can be
equals. See, they don't want us to be equals. She's just
been using me, same way that Bill's been using you. (2.7)

Once again, Sookie hears the warning but ignores it until she's
put in terrible danger.

Debbie
Sookie and Debbie Pelt dress as opposites but look similar, with
blonde fair and thin figures (though Debbie looks much
scruffier). On her werewolf pack initiation night at Lou Pine's
Biker Bar, she wears black fishnets, spiked gantlets, and not
much else. When Sookie accompanies Alcide to the bar, she
dresses like Debbie in a sexy black corset top with fake tattoos
and flirts with weres. Doing so, she discovers what it would be
like to be Debbie, so deep into the supernatural that she's
hooked on V. Debbie is season three's bad girl, and Sookie finds
herself craving a bit of bad girl in herself after Bill has just
broken up with her. Debbie left the epic romance of her life to
just have sex and fun, something Sookie wonders about. For the
one night, she dresses aggressively and hangs out with weres,
secure in the knowledge that she's brought Alcide as backup.

The Queen of Louisiana
Sophie-Ann first appears feeding on a young woman, a
subordinate she briskly dismisses. "She's like a 1940s movie
star" the director notes (Cuesta and Woo). Self-centered and
young, she dismisses the ancient, saintly Godric's death with a
simple "that blows" (2.12). Nonetheless, she has an ancient
wisdom of magical lore, and Bill and Eric both sincerely fear
her. Her movie-star-style house with its immense Roman pool
and open space suggests the ancient, uncorrupted past.
　　Sophie-Ann functions as a Shadow or foil for Sookie,
though they don't meet on the show. She's Sookie's opposite,

tugging at Bill and Eric in the opposite direction: Sookie is a human pawn in vampire schemes, Sophie-Ann is a vampire queen and the men's boss. Sookie is working-class, self-directed, and kind. "Sophie, the vampire queen of all Louisiana, can think of little better to do with her power and prestige than to hang out in a home that looks like a Barbie Dream House® and play Yahtzee® with her bored harem" (Mamatas 65). While Sookie is living, Sophie-Ann only plays at life, dwindling away her days doing nothing important. In her Malibu-style residence, Sophie-Anne lounges by a large swimming pool under a painted sky "where, in a perverse inversion of Sookie, she playacts at sunbathing" (Ruddell and Cherry 46). Both have Eric and Bill fawning over them. And Sophie-Ann holds Sookie's blonde cousin prisoner, emphasizing her villainous power. Both men must choose between her and Sookie, deciding whether the crave power or love.

Portia
Portia Bellefleur is the same age as Sookie, but she grew up in a mansion and is like the royalty of Bon Temps. A successful lawyer and professional in dark elegant dresses or power suits, she has the life Sookie never could. She's presented as a contrast to Sookie, the anti-Sookie Bill dates after their breakup. At the same time, she's only interested in sex and isn't bothered that Bill says he'll never love her. Their relationship is disturbing and incestuous, breaking more taboos than Bill and Sookie's, reminding Bill of what he's lost that can never be replaced.

Pam
Pam is the cruel, nasty voice who expresses the truth others prefer to hide. "Pam never looked happy when she was dressed like a fictional vampire. She was the real thing and proud of it" (*Dead as a Doornail* 24). As Sookie interacts with her, she learns to be independent, taking on the world while ignoring what everyone thinks. Pam dances "unself-consciously in her own dance, her unnaturally strong and limber body bending and twisting in ways human bodies couldn't" (*Dead as a Doornail* 35). This is Sookie's lesson—to become a similar force of

independence. "I discovered being a vampire freed some wild thing inside me," Pam says. "I wanted to try everything I'd been denied in my human life" (*All Together Dead* 89).

"She is a tough woman, who comes from a tough time and chose to be a vampire over 100 years ago. She is too wise and independent to let her guard down without a fight," notes Kristin Bauer van Straten (Pam) (Halterman). She's physically powerful as she withstands torture at the Magister's hands, then turns on him when she's freed. She's independent, well-traveled, sexually experienced with both genders. She's not maternal, dumping Jessica on Bill because she's "annoying" and only reluctantly giving her advice. As such, she and Sookie have opposite and complementary abilities. Under Pam's influence, Sookie's polite, good-girl side fades into the background. "I realized that my temper had been showing more and more lately. Ever since I'd gotten to know the vampires," she relates (*Club Dead* 53).

Pam's devotion to Eric also proves a counterpoint to Sookie, who knows she can't trust him. Some of Pam's conversations with Sookie echo the waitress's most complicated thoughts on the vampire sheriff.

> Pam: You really should reconsider his offer.
> Sookie: Why? So he can keep me? Use me? Drink from me? Or maybe lose control and drain me altogether?
> Pam: It beats someone else doin' it. With what you are, Faerie Princess, you need to be somebody's, or you won't be at all. Eric is handsome, he's rich, and in his own way, he cares about you. He really does.
> Sookie: Thanks for the advice. But I will never be Eric Northman's puppet.
> Pam: Mmm. Shame for you, then. He pulls good string. (4.2)

Pam reveals the truth to Sookie on more than one occasion, taking Sookie to find him having sex with the new dancer:

> Sookie: What the...?
> Eric: Sookie...see anything you like?
> Pam: I do.

Eric: I take it Sookie couldn't be stopped?
Pam: What can I say? She overpowered me. (3.1)

Here, notably, Pam says the sassy things Sookie can't, admiring Eric's body and building Sookie up as powerful. For Pam, love is forever, a lesson struggling Sookie must learn. As Pam notes:

> You humans love your pain don't you?...You promise to never forget each other, you promise to feel the sting of loss forever because for y'all forever is just the blink of an eye. Your lives are pathetically brief. When we say forever we have to mean it. (6.5)

Sookie wears Pam's clothes in the first season when "there's vampire in her cleavage." At this moment, a vampire has died on her word, and she's closer to Pam than she's ever been. By putting on her clothes, she gets to sample being a Fangtasia worker and discover what it would be like to live in that world.

Ginger is another blonde in service to Eric. She's been glamoured into a fragile shell of herself, a walking reminder of how vampires use people and how little they care.

Eric: When Ginger is finished, glamour her for me.
Pam: Are you sure? She's been glamoured one too many times already. Who's knows how much of her is left.
Eric: It's either that or turn her. You want her?
Pam: Please! I'm not that desperate. Glamour it is.
Eric: Excellent. (1.9)

Though her scenes and screams are played for comedy, she's a sad reminder of how vampire-human relationships turn out. Sookie's fairy powers protect her from glamour, but if not, she easily could have been Ginger, used and mistreated by Eric and Pam.

Unlike Ginger and Sookie, Pam is the female that Eric likes enough to turn, the blonde assistant in Eric's life as Sookie could easily become. Sookie notes that she, Pan, and Eric's book progeny Karin are three different shades of blonde, all with blue eyes and curves. "Eric ran true to type," she thinks (*Dead Ever*

After 90). She's only the latest of his conquests and the only one still human…for now. In the books, Sookie and Eric have a relationship for several novels, and she wonders what life would be like as his vampire bride. "When Eric had turned Pam and Karin, he'd gotten blond warriors," she reflects. "If I became a vampire I'd be like them. I thought of things I'd already done. I shivered" (*Dead Ever After* 90). She's already become a slayer of vampires, weres, and fairies—would life really change so much?

At the same time, Pam and Karin are Eric's victims, in service to him for all eternity, devoted without being able to help it, confined to darkness. For daylight-loving, life-loving Sookie, this would be a terrible punishment. When she tells Eric she won't agree to be turned, he grows bitter and snarls, "I should have turned you without asking as I did to Karin and Pam" (*Dead Ever After* 122). Pam and Karin are "his" in a way Sookie will never consent to become.

This shadow dynamic works both ways, as Sookie is also the intruder in Eric and Pam's exclusive relationship. "I've been with Eric over 100 years. I've watched him seduce super models and princesses and spit out their bones when he was finished. How can someone named Sookie take him away from me," Pam demands (4.12). Eric's human lovers come and go, but Pam is the permanent presence in his life, the one he values above all…until he falls in love. After season four, Sookie and Pam find themselves struggling over Eric as both have a claim to him.

When Tara is shot, Sookie realizes that the powerful female vampire is their only recourse. Pam is the one to offer dazzling vampire resurrection powers. However, Pam must learn gentleness and love from Sookie, just as Sookie must gain a backbone from Pam. Pam dons Sookie's Wall-mart sweatsuit and cradles Tara all night with an odd tenderness and honor. At this moment, Pam is sampling being Sookie, the loving maternal figure and protector of Tara. After this experience, Pam changes. She goes on to become Tara's mother, protector, and lover, as she begins a new chapter in her own life.

VALERIE ESTELLE FRANKEL

Tara

Sookie and Tara are more than friends—as a picture of the two girls posing with Grandma Adele shows, they're basically sisters. Adele was the one to give Tara a safe home and occasionally call social services on Tara's mother. Jason, too, protected Tara like a brother when her drunk mother came calling. When Tara invents a fake background for herself in New Orleans, she names Jason as her brother, suggesting a kind of wish-fulfillment. "Their friendship is…such a good core. With Gran gone from season one, you get a little of that feeling back when they're together," notes Deborah Ann Woll (Jessica).

Same-sex siblings tend to be both Shadow and ideal self for each other. As Jungian analyst Christine Downing puts it, "She is both what I would most aspire to be but feel I never can be *and* what I am most proud *not* to be but fearful of becoming" (111). Tara is "smart and active but grating, damaged, and abused" (Mukherjea 120). She envies Sookie's family and stability, while Sookie envies Tara's independence and forcefulness.

Siblings in real life tend to polarize, half-consciously dividing attributes like "I'm the bright one and she's the pretty one" (Downing 111). Likewise, in fiction, they're usually opposites to draw attention to their differences and emphasize their roles as different characters. Tara and Sookie are no exception. They usually dress in contrasting colors: one in purple, one in yellow, or one in blue and one in pink. Of course, their physical and emotional differences also contrast: Sookie is known for being sweet, while Tara's anger is her most famous feature. "Because Tara is so reactionary—often to a cringe-worthy extent—Sookie ends up looking rooted when she talks to her friend" (Wilcott 100). Sookie keeps all the town's secrets, while Tara says everything she thinks. Tara wears her long dark hair down, Sookie's is shorter, blonde, and usually up. Sookie has a stable house, Tara drifts.

Tara prefers to attack society as she shows in her first appearance—standing up for herself outweighs keeping her job or fitting in. Jason, the brother of this family, follows the rules as he fashions his public persona—ladies' man, road crew, sports hero. Sookie by contrast is eager to subtly break conventions to the point of dating vampires and occasionally spooking people with her mind reading.

Their quests also contrast—in the first season, Bill and Sookie commence their epic love, while Tara and Sam try occasional loveless hookups. In seasons two and three, Tara is trying to escape that dark power that holds her captive, while Sookie is trying to break in and rescue her friends. In season four, Tara willingly submits to the dark power of the wiccans. While Sookie has come through her experiences and remained upbeat, Tara is traumatized and consumed by a need for revenge so great that she's prepared to see all the vampires burn. Season five, Tara becomes a vampire—the thing she hates most, and once more, Sookie is the one who must reach out to her.

"Both Sookie and Tara are intelligent women who work in service industry jobs. It makes sense that with their similar backgrounds, they would have similar roles. But Sookie has certain privileges because she is white that Tara does not" (Craton and Jonell 112). Tara is assumed to have a baby-daddy, and characters from Maryann to Franklin decide to use her, while men keep their respectful distance from Sookie (admittedly, mostly because of her telepathy). More importantly, Sookie has supportive family—her loving grandmother rather than Tara's abusive mother.

Sookie also has body independence—she isn't taken over by vampires or demonic pregnancies or possession—her power, her "light" comes from within. By contrast, Tara is possessed by the Maenad, raped by Franklin, and then shot and turned by the predatory females of the series, all against her will. When she becomes a vampire, Pam tries to encourage her to be whoever she wants. But soon enough they're on the run and then locked in the governor's "camp." Once again, Sookie is free and in love while Tara is trapped by powerful forces. Nonetheless, Tara remains a constant cautionary tale—she is Sookie if Sookie gives in to rage and hate. She is used by Franklin as Sookie could be used by Bill, seduced by Maryann and Marnie as Sookie could be by the forces of darkness.

In romance, Sookie falls in love with all her heart and soul, and Bill and Eric clearly love her in return. In between their own relationships, Sam and Alcide are also devoted to her. By contrast, Tara attempts a "just-physical" relationship with Sam, and then loses love interests Eggs and Naomi the kickboxer because Maryann forces Eggs to do such terrible things that he can't live with himself and then because Naomi is in danger. In between these is Franklin, the vampire who rapes and kidnaps Tara. In the books, Franklin is a rich, generous gentleman vampire, but he passes Tara to the brutish Mickey, who insists, "Tara doesn't need anything but me, until I'm tired of her" (*Dead as a Doornail* 163). With a far weaker book Tara unable to kill him, Sookie must intervene by calling in the vampire cavalry.

After her transformation on the show, Tara sparks with Pam, but their constant death threats as they wage war against the American government, combined with their complex maker-child relationship makes their romance problematic. Tara's romances are all tragedies that leave her miserable and traumatized. "Tara had been through a lot in her life and she was a tough, if wounded, bird" Sookie acknowledges admiringly (*Club Dead* 161). While Sookie embraces life and love, Tara has been marked for death.

Facing the Chaotic Shadow
In the second season, Sookie travels to Dallas and enters the Belly of the Beast as Campbell calls it—the enemy's lair in the underground cells of the Church of the Sun. The force of the misogynistic patriarchy, who clings to the fundamentalist ways of rhetoric and intolerance, rules there. However, the patriarchy is dangerously ignorant. A fundamental lack of understanding defines them, as they insist vampires are unnatural and turn their backs on those who support them. Reverend Newlin believes he captured Godric through his own skill, not that Godric allowed it. He also believes he and his teenage boys with wooden weapons can defeat the vampires. However, they only practice with props and actors. They are a church preaching hate and filled with hypocrisy—the reverend's wife cheats on him, they imprison Sookie and Godric, they turn on their trusting informant. While they consider themselves on the side of God

and humanity, they're caught up with personal vengeance.

When Eric and his fellows show up, Reverend Newlin is revealed as an empty authority, one whose followers won't die for his cause. With the aid of the enlightened male, Godric, the evil church leader is not killed, merely stripped of his authority and left defeated.

On the heroine's journey, the heroine sees the powerful patriarch die and realizes he is not the powerful force she had once thought. The heroine is the one with the story's power, though she must determine how to use it.

> Dorothy cowers before the "Great and Powerful Oz" when she reaches his Emerald City. But after facing the far more terrifying Wicked Witch of the West, she grows into someone strong enough to kick over the Wizard's pasteboard head and confront the fraud cowering behind it. Katniss too realizes that the Capitol's threat far outweighs the Capitol itself. As she declares on one of her broadcasts: "The Capitol's fragile because it depends on the districts for everything. Food, energy, even the Peacekeepers that police us. If we declare our freedom, the Capitol collapses. President Snow, thanks to you, I'm officially declaring mine today" (*MJ* 169). Like their broken electric fences, the Capitol has only the illusion of authority, until Katniss can shatter it. At series end, she meets Snow heavily shackled and helpless in his rose garden and knows she can kill him. (Frankel, *Katniss* 121)

Likewise, Sookie sees the church shatter, and then witnesses Godric's death. With the male church structure and the vampire patriarch both dead, Sookie can take power on her own quest.

In contrast, Maryann's household "calls to mind the nurturing and communal mentality of feminist conscious-raising groups" (Craton and Jonell 114). However, Maryann's agenda is insane. As Sookie's adversary, Maryann "highlights the risk that uninhibited sexuality poses to society and how it can become a source of violence between men and women" (Craton and Jonell 114). As Sookie deals with romantic vampires and weres, this is a lesson she must learn. Thus, the youthful heroine is pitted against the dark savage feminine, whom she must confront to learn from in the classic heroine's journey arc. When Maryann takes over Sookie's house with her mad emotional power, encouraging celebration over reason, Sookie determines to stop her.

After her induction into the dark, greedy, uncontrolled side of romance beside Hugo the traitor and Eric, who tricks her into drinking his blood, Sookie descends into the Maenad's den of vice. As she tells Lafayette, "My Gran lived and died in that house, and now it's like people who are the exact opposite of everything she was are...defiling her. I almost got raped in Dallas, but this is so much worse" (2.11).

This mindless violence has entered her inner sanctum as the far-off violence in Dallas did not. Houses represent selves, and Sookie's house has been filled with debauchery. This actually reflects Sookie's inner self, suddenly whirling with lustful thoughts of Eric. It's no coincidence that she faces the place beside Lafayette, who's also drunk Eric's blood and is dealing with the effects. Both are dealing with the larger supernatural world and the pull of strange longings, all brought about by Eric, the trickster force who upsets the status quo. However, though Lafayette trembles from his trauma and Maryann takes him over, she doesn't get Sookie. With a cry of, "I am not weak, and I am not afraid. I am gonna kick that bitch's evil ass out of my Gran's house and then you are gonna shoot her," Sookie descends into the pit (2.11).

Everyone there indulges in the behaviors their daylight selves are afraid to try: Terry and Arlene fall in love, Sherriff Dearborne dances around in his underwear. However, Lafayette, Jason, and Andy, recently returned from their own personal pits, hold out a bit longer—they've faced their demons so they're less off guard when confronted by them. It's the wholly innocent characters who have more trouble.

Bon Temps is seething with hatred, resentment, prejudice, and fear. In fact Sookie the telepath experiences it all on a daily basis, though most of the others in Bon Temps bottle it up, continuing their proper behavior and emphasizing that they're decent people. "Responsible people try so hard to be good all the time—when they get a taste of being bad, they can't get enough. It's like—kablooey!" the vengeance demon Anya explains on *Buffy* ("Smashed"). As Daphne the shifter describes the Maenad life, "It's really just a kind of energy. Wild energy, like lust, anger, excess, violence. Basically all the fun stuff" (2.7). That's exactly what the town is craving.

Estés adds, "When a woman agrees to becomes too 'well-bred' her instincts for these [wild] impulses drop down into her darkest unconscious, outside her automatic reach" (233). Someone like Hoyt's mother thus loses control, craving sex, violence, and any sort of misbehavior as a release. In this case, the entire town, fed up with repressing their racist attitudes, anger at the vampires, and polite behavior, turns savage. When a person is always well-behaved, he or she is not taking the time to feel anger and moodiness, to connect with the hidden Shadow side that represses these emotions. Thus the Shadow can unexpectedly take over the entire personality.

Michelle Forbes, Maryann's actress, said season two was an allegory for "pack mentality thinking"—doing violence or other extreme acts because everyone else is (O'Connor). Indeed, pack mentality takes over, especially in the scenes when the entire crowd decides to murder Sam.

> By the end of the season, we had seen things break: the foundations of beliefs (Jason's), of normality (Maryann), of relationships (Sookie and Bill). Intruders gained ground (Eric in Sookie's dreams; Maryann at Merlotte's), and things and people we thought stable became lost or began to fall apart (Godric, Andy Bellefleur). (Lima 41)

Lafayette returned from his basement imprisonment a shell of himself, and Tara lost her mind under Maryann's influence. Daphne the were-waitress was another disruption as she messed up all the orders then finally betrayed Sam. From her heart removal to Miss Jeanette's in Merlotte's parking lot, the atmosphere of Merlotte's grew darker as the bar lost its heart.

After, the people blame everything from bad vodka to an alien invasion. They laugh off the concept that such darkness and frenzy dwells inside all of them. In fact, only Eggs seeks the truth of what happened, and finding the answer devastates him.

The night is treated as a time of drunken excess, easily laughed off. There is a joy and peace in letting go and surrendering to the wild senses:

> Maryann: What about the mystics of every religion?
> Eggs: What about them?
> Maryann: They would black out. Run and dance through the streets, levitate, act like monkeys, run around naked. Everybody thought they were crazy.
> Tara: They were crazy.
> Maryann: No, Tara. They were ecstatic. All that fake civilization bullshit just fell away so they could dissolve into the infinite, so they could lose themselves and unite with their god. (2.9)

This is also the side of the self that prim Sookie has never embraced. However, after her adventure with the Church of the Sun, it's waiting for her, consuming her family home. Every buried impulse, everything she hasn't faced, lurks here, beckoning to her. All in white down to her soft slippers, Sookie descends into the once-innocent farmhouse, now filled with lust, gluttony, and mayhem. On the floor, Mike Spencer drags her onto the floor and holds her down in the filth.

> Mike: Remember when your Gran was layin' here... all bloody and dead?
> Sookie: Of course I do.
> Mike: Come on down here with me...Makes me feel more alive bein' in the presence of death, don't it? Well, I guess you'd know that.
> Sookie: Not as much as you.
> Mike: How come you let him put his dead pecker inside you? It ain't natural and I ain't right.
> Sookie: I don't think you're in any position to talk about what's natural and right. (2.11)

Sookie willingly lies down beside him and faces the dark truths she doesn't admit about her relationship with Bill. She then participates in the dark lustful fantasy to trick the man, saying, "Mike, enough with the foreplay. Let's just... let's just do it already. On one condition. I have to be on top." Then she hits him with a frying pan.

To conquer the underworld one cannot cower in fear; one must take its dark energy and use it, allow one's nasty vicious strong side out. That's the only way to defeat the underworld's strength.

Maryann's wedding is corrupted in every aspect, like Sookie's house. Maryann wears Grandma Adele's wedding dress, which finally houses her shriveled blackened corpse. The wedding feast is a pile of dead animals. As maid of honor, Sookie is tied up and threatened with her brother's death. The bridesmaids must lick blood onto a white egg, symbol of fertility and life. "The egg-licking...It's a sort of twisted, maenad version of one of those inane bridal shower games that you have to play," the script writer revealed (Cuesta and Woo 2.12). Everything is skewed and twisted. "We scripted like, the most disturbing version of Mendleson's wedding march," she added.

As the shadow, Maryann says things Sookie has always feared and sublimated.

> Sookie: You have no right to wear that dress.
> Maryann: I know I should have asked, but I couldn't find you. You'll probably never use it anyway. (2.12)

As her actress notes, "She's not afraid. She can eat what she likes, she can have sex with whom she likes, she can play with whom she likes. She can dress in beautiful clothes. She has everything at her fingertips. There's nothing she doesn't need" (O'Connor). As such, she's everything Sookie's ever wanted to be but can't. "Her rage to sacrifice Sam Merlotte fits the stereotype of the feminist as man-eater" (Craton and Jonell 114). Sookie, by contrast, is the youthful savior.

Maryann also pushes her to use her powers.

> Maryann: I'm all yours. Give it your best.
> Sookie: My best what?
> Maryann: The electricity. Do it again.
> Sookie: I can't. It's never happened to me before. I don't even know what it was.

> Maryann: I never felt anything like it. It was like nature herself was shooting out from your fingertips.
> [Sookie tries.]
> Maryann: That's hitting me. You're not committing to this at all.
> Sookie: I do not have electrical powers. I am a human being.
> Maryann: You keep saying that. But if you were human... I would have taken you over by now. Come on. It'll be our little secret. What are you? (2.12)

With this exchange, Maryann reveals the truth to Sookie—she is more than human. She has an amazing electrical power, making her a nature goddess herself. Maryann too has an electrical power, as she feeds off others' chaos and ecstasy. Of course, hers is a power of wildness, while Sookie stuns enemies into stillness. This force of feminine underworld power and chaos provokes Sookie to find the same power within herself, to channel her inner dark goddess. As Silvia Brinton Perera comments in *Descent to the Goddess,* "Until the demonic powers of the dark Goddess are claimed, there is not strength in the woman to grow from daughter to an adult who can stand against the force of patriarchy" (42).

Once again, the helpful males in Sookie's life aid her—Sam and Bill, representing her rational side—work together to trick the maenad and break her into pieces...literally. With the Maenad's death, Sookie's halves, the woodsman Sam and aristocratic Bill, make their peace and come to understand they both care about Sookie and the town, and that they trust each other. A quarrel deep inside Sookie is symbolically resolved.

Sookie vs Lorena
Season two ends with Bill's proposal and Sookie's conflicted confusion. Marriage is often a sacrificial act, losing the self for a new shared identity (Pearson and Pope 36). The goal for the heroine is to keep one's self intact within the union and not be consumed.

As Sookie spends more and more time with Bill, he's absorbing her entire life. He drinks her blood, he drags her to

Fangtasia for extra jobs, he leaves her a stepdaughter to babysit. Sam is unsurprised when Sookie bails on her work again to go hunt down her boyfriend. As she changes from Sam's employee to Eric's (at least temporarily), cares for Jessica not Tara, and leaves Bon Temps altogether, her old life is being replaced by a vampiric one. She spends more time with Bill than with Tara, leaving for half a season as her grandmother's house was possessed, like most of her town, friends, and family. If she continues with Bill, all these aspects of her life will become as neglected as her house became. With him, she cannot become a mother or even discover an independent life. Her mysterious origins also pull at her: Sookie has trouble accepting his proposal since "I'm not even sure what I am," as she puts it (2.12).

Lorena and her cronies represent the Shadow antagonist but also a protective force in Sookie's life as the dark feminine like Maryann who forces her to grow. They act on Sookie's confusion by protecting her from herself—they steal Bill from Sookie before she can accept.

In the book, Sookie asks Eric to put a hit on Lorena and adds, "If she were a human, I'd take care of it myself" (*Club Dead* 53). After, she wonders to herself how she became so violent, noting, "There was something pretty savage inside me, and I'd always controlled it" (*Club Dead* 53). Lorena is the dark savage feminine lover, an aspect of herself sweet Sookie has never explored. Lorena, in a reversal of traditional gender roles, treats Bill like a type of mistress/subordinate whom she dominates in various ways. However, Sookie is evoking that commanding dark lover in herself as she faces it in the other woman.

Seeking Bill, Sookie journeys into a were club, encountering others' rage and violence. She also meets Alcide and Debbie, a couple just as mismatched and problematic as she is with Bill. Alcide's sister describes the pairing in a way that brings home to Sookie exactly how she's been living: "She was his first love, he never met anybody so alive, all that shit. But how many bullets are you gonna take for somebody? How many bad things gotta happen to you and the ones you love before you realize feeling alive ain't enough? I am just glad he made it out alive" (3.4). For Sookie, there's no such guarantee. "Vampires often turn on those they love the most," Bill notes later (5.12). At the same time, Alcide, the generous, noble male presence, reminds her she can have relationships and male helpers other than a great star-crossed romance.

Bill calls Sookie and breaks up with her, devastating her further. "I am death. I will bring you only suffering. Our worlds are too different. Our natures too. We were doomed from the start," he says, echoing the thoughts she's had on gloomy nights (3.4).

At last, Sookie enters the king of Louisiana's mansion, a place where she has no power and is locked in her room like a princess in a tower. The other female protagonist, Tara, is trapped there by Franklin, raped repeatedly and soon to lose her humanity. "Russell's house is reminiscent of an aristocratic European dwelling signifying the height of wealth and power" (Ruddell and Cherry 46). This is an all-male place where Sookie has few allies.

Typically, Lorena wears adult black or burgundy, upscale beaded gowns in contrast with Sookie's sundresses and shorts. When they meet in the mansion, Lorena dresses in Sookie's color, white, emphasizing her role as Bill's other woman. There, Lorena feeds off Sookie, marring her white gown with Sookie's blood.

After this mixing of dark strength, Sookie gains the dark power and rage to snatch a stake and use it. When Lorena says, "William, I love you," Sookie cries, "You wouldn't know love if it kicked you in the fangs," and stakes her, killing her claim over Bill (3.7). Sookie rises from Lorena's body, pale dress sprayed with blood just like Lorena's. She gains the strength to root around in Lorena's guts for the manacle key and drag Bill away. In the book, she notes, "I began talking to him under my breath, cursing him…telling him I would beat him up if he didn't make it to the car" (*Club Dead* 209). Facing Lorena has given her a new mother-bear strength, one that fills her with the strength to save Bill, to slice her arm and offer her blood like vampires do.

However, her relationship with Bill has been marred forever

by his rejection. He is revealed as the frightening, savage side of his vampire nature. He turns into a ravening, mindless monster, something he's been all along under a cloak of civilization. "While the romantic lover's power to save the female hero is seriously undercut in modern literature, his power to destroy women becomes more obvious" (Pearson and Pope 36). Love is dangerous, and Sookie's love for Bill could destroy her.

He feeds on her, taking far too much. In the book, he rapes her as well, an act Sookie knows she cannot forgive. "Now the naive self has knowledge about a killing force loose within the psyche," Estés explains (55). On the show, he drains her until she falls into a coma. Loving, sweet Sookie collapses, near death, but her powerful best friend steps in for her. Tara flings Bill into the sunlight to die and gets Sookie to the hospital. She calls Jason, and Sookie's friends all rally around her, to help in every way they can imagine. With the lover revealed as predator and cast out of her life, the other parts of her personality, from Lafayette's brashness to Jason's befuddled love, return.

"Today, it is generally understood that the romantic and spiritual man-god—the male ideal worthy of a woman's self-sacrifice and worship, for whom she is expected to set aside herself and her life—simply does not exist, except in myth" (Pearson and Pope 35). Sookie must build a life for herself without Bill by fulfilling her true quest and learning who she is.

In the same episode that Bill feeds on Sookie, Sookie has a death and rebirth sequence. Her relationship is ending, but she is preparing for something better. She's transported to a vision of pink gauze and rose petals, a sanctuary of the feminine that will keep her safe from the devouring masculine, who will drink her dry if she allows it. When Claudine reveals herself and cautions Sookie "He will steal your light" (3.7), she is acting to protect Sookie from the now-revealed threat just as Tara is.

At season end, Sookie considers reconciling with Bill. Immediately Eric arrives to reveal Bill has lied to her from their first meeting—he's actually a predator sent to kill her. Once again, the friends have stepped in to save Sookie from herself. Sookie dumps him. After, Bill retreats into the masculine world of power and hierarchy, slaying the queen and taking her job as king of Louisiana. Sookie retreats into the feminine world, fairyland.

The characters around her also have breakups and closure of various sorts, reflecting her devastating parting from Bill: Alcide kills Debbie's boyfriend and leaves Debbie behind. Eric and the king and queen kill the Magister and declare themselves the new authority. Tommy robs Sam and Sam shoots Tommy, both crossing a line in their relationship. Like Sookie, none of them will be the same.

The Shapeshifter
The heroine's journey usually contains a beauty and the beast tale, as her ideal love is a shapeshifter. This, like everything else, is a metaphor for part of the human psyche. "We have all experienced relationships in which our partner is fickle, two-faced, bewilderingly changeable," Vogler explains (65). This shapeshifter-lover is a mystery for the heroine to crack as she chooses what she wants in life. It's no coincidence that Sookie's potential boyfriends are shifters, weres, and vampires, hiding deep secrets.

All vampires, switching between human face and vampire fangs, between trying to pass and feeding off the innocent, are cast as shapeshifters in fiction. "The vampire represents the unity of opposites, a boundary breaker: male/female, good/bad, dead/alive; they defy the categories and constraints of culture. They offer the potential for a liminal space, in which contradictions and critiques can be worked through," notes Gina Wisker in "Vampires and School Girls."

The vampire refuses to conform to social standards—an even more enormous divide in Victorian times when the genre was first popularized. In a world of polite behavior, the vampire was the creature of the night who slunk into homes and seduced young women. This is the source of his "Otherness," and thus his modern attraction. "There has been increasing emphasis on the positive aspects of the vampire's eroticism and on his or her right to rebel against the stultifying constraints of society" (Senf 163).

Bill is a shapeshifter, and like many series, he offers the

heroine a beauty-and-the-beast relationship. He is the prince, certainly, cultured and sophisticated, with old world charm and skill at removing petticoats. He treats Sookie like a lady in a world in which she's only a waitress. However, he's also a blood-drinking monster. When Bill hears a mob killed the other vampires in the first book, his savagery appears and he attacks Sookie. She relates:

> I could feel his anger.
> I could feel his cruelty.
> I could feel his hunger.
> He had never been more completely vampire. There wasn't anything human in him. (*Dead Until Dark* 180)

Though Sookie may claim Bill is a "good" vampire, filled with morality, she's drawn to him because of his darkness— something she's never developed in herself. On the show, we watch him savage people beside Lorena, glamour a cop and fill him with terror, and execute Sookie's uncle. Later of course she falls for Eric, who isn't restrained by morality. These dark, murderous vampires call to her, bad boys to her good girl self.

Eric, even more than Bill, is the obvious dissembler. As Bill points out, "Eric has had a thousand years practicing deceit." In one of his more important tricks, he persuades Sookie he'll die if she doesn't drink his blood and thus he forms a bond between them. Bill adds, "He lied to prove his power to me. He counted on your goodness, there's no shame in that" (2.9). Eric also tells devastating truths Sookie doesn't want to hear:

> Eric: The first time Bill declared you his, how did it make you feel?
> Sookie: Angry.
> Eric: But safe? (4.2)

He has a pointed way of looking at situations. "To have and to hold, to love and to cherish, to blah, blah, blah, blah, blah, until death do you part. Doesn't bother you that you'll be the only one dying?" (3.2).

"One minute you lie to me, the next minute you ask me to

trust you. You do something generous and selfless, and then you follow that up with something nasty or downright cruel," Sookie complains (3.2). In that scene, Eric has arrived at her house to offer her secrets but also to threaten and flirt. It's no wonder she's bewildered by him. Her only guarantee is that none of his moods, helpful or hurtful, will last long.

While Bill is single-minded and uncompromising (especially when negotiating with fellow vampires such as the King of Mississippi or Queen of Louisiana), Eric is more flexible. He pretends to be a member of the Church of the Sun to sneak in and rescue Godric, and he "plays the game" of being a friendly "small business owner" and vampire spokesperson on camera (4.1). He also has a number of costumes. We've seen him as a Viking and a Nazi. He disguises himself as a guard in season six to sneak through the government-run camp, dressing Willa in a scientist's labcoat. In the second season, he completely changes his look, cutting off his blood-drenched hair and experimenting with a roguishly unzipped tracksuit. When Sookie hears Eric called the sheriff she pictures him with a silver star or "in black tights as the villainous sheriff of Nottingham" (*Dead to the World* 224).

In the third book, he pretends to be Alcide's old friend, with a suit, ponytail braid, and glasses. Sookie decides he's ready for vampire *GQ*. Later, he negotiates with the king's people over the phone. "Suddenly he had an English accent. Mr. Master of Disguise," Sookie thinks (*Club Dead* 233). He also climbs into bed with Sookie and she mistakes him for Bill, in another instance of his shapeshifting.

Eric's glee at his amorality keeps him comic, lighthearted even in the midst of cruelty and viciousness. He's happy being a sheriff who manipulates the stately kings, the underdog subverting the great Authority. As Lewis Hyde describes the classic trickster figure, "He doesn't win the way the big guys do, but he doesn't suffer the way they do, either, and he enjoys pleasures they find too risky" (342). The pleasure he wants is Sookie, and he keeps after her with low grade mischief—he doesn't assault her, but he does lock her in his basement *after* she's come to visit. He buys her house legitimately and refits it with his own cubbyhole. He doesn't steal her blood, but he convinces her to drink his. "Although the trickster does things that benefit people, he [...] is also an impulsive, selfish, even grotesque character who steals food, tricks women into sex, and casually profanes sacred rituals" (Garry and El-Shamy).

Whether rewards or punishments will most easily get him what he wants, that's fine with Eric. He chains Lafayette in his basement and tortures him, then later offers him a sports car (though not the insurance—he's not stupid as he puts it). He genuinely loves Pam and Sookie (in different ways) but responds to Sookie with a teasing immaturity she finds maddening. He's much more playful than somber Bill.

The Trickster's main function as the natural enemy of the status quo is to "bring about healthy change and transformation, often by drawing attention to the imbalance or absurdity of a stagnant psychological situation," Vogler explains (77). Eric, like other tricksters, is a catalyst for others' darkness. He reminds Sookie how little Bill has to offer, then permanently breaks them up with the truth that Sookie's first meeting with Bill was a setup. He is the one to coax Sookie to drink his blood recreationally, something Bill never tries. Under his own spell, Eric drains Sookie's useless, alluring godmother of her false beauty and her power, turning her into a shriveled corpse.

In season four, they fall in love at last. Eric has undergone his greatest shift—from bossy vampire sheriff to helpless dependent. The new Eric stands half-naked in the woods, expression lost and confused. He's humbly grateful for all of Sookie's help. When he gets drunk on fairy blood, he goes through another personality change. After, he's depressed and Sookie finds herself seeing many more sides to him, all honest, loving, and needy.

Good Witch, Bad Witch: Holly and Marnie

> Holly: Black cohosh. Brings down your testosterone levels. For your rage. You obviously have a problem.
> Sam: Thanks. You got anything that works for nosiness and bad boundaries?

> Holly: Oh, I'm sorry. It's just something I do. I give people remedies. I'm a Wiccan. (3.10)

In Holly Cleary's early appearances, she's an adoptive mother to those at the bar: She takes Tara to a rape support group and offers to help Arlene get an abortion if she wants one. She offers affection to the conflicted, drug-ridden Andy Bellefleur, and comfort to Sookie.

The holly plant was used to bring blessings and as an evergreen symbol of everlasting life (Shepherd 245). Her last name, Cleary, comes from "clear," indicating that she has special insight and clarity. At season four's end, she dresses as a fairy godmother, and that's how she acts toward Sookie, Tara, and Andy, helping them all to banish Marnie.

Marnie is the enemy of the vampires, and soon, of Tara, Holly, and Sookie as well. She begins as a frumpy, harmless elderly woman without a solid grasp on reality, unable to accept that the vampires will slaughter her and all her friends. Marnie, like Sophie-Ann, is heavily in denial. Both believe problems will go away if they aren't dealt with.

> Marnie: He had no right to approach us. It's his fault. This is a sacred space.
> Tara: Nothing is sacred to them.
> Marnie: Well, the Goddess. She will protect us…Go away. Just go away. People are so violent, and so perplexing. Just leave me alone with the dead. (4.4)

She naively thinks the vampires will be stopped by the Bill of Rights' freedom of religion guarantee, while a traumatized Lafayette warns her the vampires have their own code of justice.

The wiccan group at Moongoddess Emporium represents a female power structure, with a circle meeting to seek inner spirituality not outer power. Instantly the vampires see them as a threat when their life power potentially threatens vampirekind:

> Bill: They're necromancers, Eric. They brought a bird back from the dead.
> Eric: Are you certain of this?

Bill: I had someone on the inside. I hope I don't have to impress upon you the implications of this.
Eric: You do not.
Bill: If they can control the dead, then they can control us. (4.2)

The emphasis here is on power and force. After Eric delivers a brutal ultimatum, Marnie comments, shocked, that she and her friends had no plans to harm anyone and only wanted to practice their religion. The clichéd masculine thought process, obsessed with dominance, meets the clichéd feminine thought process, naively asserting its freedom without thought to the power structure. A war ensues. Eric nearly drains Marnie, and, bullied and victimized, she snaps and curses him, then seeks true power for herself. She's another polite person fed up with being polite, eager to devour the dark feminine power she's never had.

"All my entire life I have wanted to mean something, to know for once and for all why I was born with one foot in the other world. Make me your servant, I beg you," she cries as she summons Antonia (4.3). Antonia is all Marnie wishes to be. As Marnie relates:

All my life I've been afraid...dead people murmuring in my ears...a creepy pathetic terrified mess moaning to herself in the corner... I'm not afraid anymore. I've got real power now. (4.12)

Thus she seizes the chance to become Antonia, the witch no one will ever dismiss again. She can rule the world, and she does, burning vampires in the sun.

Antonia begins their acquaintance with the certainty and fierceness Marnie's always sought. She proclaims:

At least in our time, they stayed hidden. Now they walk among us shameless in their lust, their hunger. They laugh at the miracle of life. We must restore the sacred power of creation to this wounded earth. That is our only hope. Snuff them out, once and for all. (4.8)

Under her influence, Marnie becomes who she's always wished, until Jesus no longer recognizes his kind friend under the witch on a power trip.

In a world where Bill is threatening to kill Sookie's new love Eric and nearly goes through with it, Sookie finds herself envying Marnie's power over vampires. She says things Sookie wishers she was powerful enough to say as she tells a rotting Pam, "Don't laugh too much. Wouldn't want your lips to fall off" (4.11).

However, Marnie has attacked Sookie's friends Eric and Tara, and is holding innocent hostages. As such, Sookie feels driven to rescue them. Her presence protects Tara from the vampires' plans to bomb Moongoddess Emporium, and her cleverness frees her friends at last. Though Marnie decides she doesn't care about human life, even stabbing a girl who tries to leave the coven, Sookie will always be protector of the helpless. Once again, Sookie descends into the enemy stronghold and battles with light, trickery, and cleverness to protect her friends. Once more she wins and banishes the dark feminine from Bon Temps.

Nonetheless, Marnie has given Sookie an important gift. She is the one to enchant Eric, turning him into a "goofy innocent Eric" Sookie can let herself love. She's acting on a lonely Sookie's secret desires, offering her a boyfriend who truly needs her, instead of the high-handed, pushy vampires she's endured in the past. Marnie is also the catalyst for the women of the story to discover the magic they can accomplish together.

> Holly: There ain't no spell that can't be undone if you got the juice. Marnie or Antonia is just another witch…She ain't no more pissed off than I am. You?
> Tara: Yeah, I got some rage!
> Holly: We are strong, angry women Tara. All we have to do is force a crack in her wall. (4.10)

Without Marnie, Sookie also wouldn't have met her Gran again, as she and Holly summon their beloved spirits to defend them. "Being alone ain't anything to be afraid of, my Sookie. We're all alone at the end," Adele tells her, after she warns that "goofy Eric" is only temporary (4.12). She's still guardian of Sookie's heart.

Good Boy or Bad Boy

> In fact, it is my opinion that everyone should choose the nice guy when it comes to a life partner. The heady, dangerous guy isn't going to pick you up on time, bring you flowers, or be the loving father you've always dreamed of…But that's in reality, folks, and if there's anything True Blood isn't, it's reality. (Rubin 19)

At first, Sookie is drawn to Bill because he's different—he's a stranger in prosaic Bon Temps, he is Other, and he offers her a silence and peace she's never found in human minds. Further, as a vampire, he's a forbidden bad boy type.

In her world of country bumpkins, he's a Southern gentleman who remembers what being a gentleman once meant. He asks to call on Sookie and charms her grandmother before sweeping Sookie off her feet as well. "Even as he was behaving gentlemanly on the surface by asking her for dates and begging her permission for a kiss, his body language was predatory, and he manhandled her a bit. There was little doubt that he was all man, albeit a dead one," notes Jonna Rubin in "SOOKEH! Bee-ill! and the Downfall of William T. Compton: How Vampire Bill Went From Sex Symbol to Sad Punchline" (24).

He has his bad boy side as he glamours a police officer and makes him hand over his gun, excusing himself to Sookie that he's being one of the "nicer" vampires. He has a five-o'clock shadow, mussed hair, and somewhat battered clothes. "He exudes casual confidence, harkening back to a time well before metrosexuals came onto the scene, when a man getting a pedicure was an action punishable by death" (Rubin 22). She meets him by running through the graveyard (or has encounters with him there) and he only shows up after dark—they're the products of their two worlds, dark and light. The entire world is against them, so they can begin their tale as star-crossed lovers.

"Season two's Bill is a little more groomed, but instead of working for him, the look is so buttoned up, it's almost stifling"

(Rubin 23). He's turned from mysterious, alluring creature of the night to the inept sudden dad who doesn't get modern-day life. He plays Wii golf and goes around bellowing "Sookie!" in his Southern accent, but he spends every episode begging her forgiveness for something ill-considered he did or a secret he's been keeping. It gets tiring. He also becomes increasingly useless at rescuing her. He fails to arrive at the Church of the Sun in time, and season three, she spends all her time rescuing him.

> Bill: Here I am, responsible for you and Jessica . . . and yet no decisions are mine. It makes me feel...
> Sookie: Like a human?
> Bill: Like a waitress (2.5)

Oh, that's attractive.

While the pair didn't last beyond season three, actors Stephen Moyer and Anna Paquin's relationship was more successful. The couple married in August 2010 after meeting on the set of the TV series in 2007. In September 2012, they had twins, a boy and a girl.

After her journey to fairyland, Sookie becomes more assertive and stronger. Her new match is the suddenly innocent and pitiful Eric-without-memories—now she is the capable guide to the supernatural, as Bill once was for her.

The new Eric is clingy and dependent. He's also a kind of amoral and indifferent that Sookie finds she secretly craves.

> Eric: Let's just leave this place while we still can.
> Sookie: This is my home and we cannot just leave Bill to die, it's not right.
> Eric: There is no right or wrong, these are human notions.
> Sookie: And I am human mostly and so were you and I've never seen you as human as you've been these past few days; it's what I've fallen in love with. But you're also a warrior, you don't run from a fight. You'd never forgive yourself.
> Eric: I just want to be with you, only you. Forever. (4.8)

It's terribly tempting not to be the savior of the world but merely become a normal couple in love. With Eric, she takes V recreationally and just has fun without Bill's dark angst. It's freeing and delightful. Eric's "full of joie de vivre—or maybe I should say joie de morte," she notes (*Dead Ever After* 130). And he's still a bad boy. "I've always said remember Eric's a vampire, vampires kill people, and I thought I had made it clear that his first choice was always going to be himself," Harris comments (Tyley, "Charlaine Harris on Death Threats").

Sookie still feels Bill's pull along with his constant jealousy. Rather than feeling tormented, however, a strong Sookie rises above it all. In a romantic red silky robe and high heels, Sookie dreams of confronting Bill and Eric and forcing them both to make peace. As she tells them:

> "I've always been this self-conscious, good little girl who's too scared to think outside the box, especially in terms of love and sex. But as of right now I'm putting this little girl behind me...I do not have to be yours or yours. I'm proposing that the two of you be mine" (4.9).

They both begin to kiss her and drink her blood, equally loving and enthusiastic.

At season end, Eric and Bill sit beside Sookie, sharing her blood and affection equally in the real world. It's a balance, one that increases her personal power and sense of self, but leaves her too divided for a single romance. "I can't stand this anymore. It's like being ripped in half. No matter what I do, somebody gets hurt," Sookie frets (4.12). Bill was her first love, but Eric with his memories is also a powerful draw. "It wasn't just goofy innocent Eric I fell for. As vicious and untrustworthy as you can be, there's a goodness in you that breaks my heart because some part of me has always wanted you," she tells him (4.12). Sookie "can't make her mind up and doesn't want anyone to be hurt, so she's walking away. It's horrible and painful and sad," Anna Paquin (Sookie) explains when she comments on the episode. "But she's never had a chance to stand on her own as a real grown-up. She's giving it a go on her own" (Keveney, "'True Blood' Sinks its Teeth").

"Sookie's had a tremendous amount of loss, so I think her trying to find family and deep profound connection with men in her life is understandable," Raelle Tucker, the episode's writer, comments. For the first time, Sookie is no longer linked to Bill or Eric. She's lost her grandmother and parents and in the same episode, she loses her best friend when Tara takes Debbie's bullet for her. At last, she's reached independence and can decide what she wants when she no longer belongs to anyone.

"The returned hero delights in a sense of wholeness and autonomy and therefore is not lonely when solitary" (Pearson and Pope 229). Season five, she seems happy without a man as she learns about the feminine world of the fairies, while Bill and Eric work their way through the Authority and its male hierarchy, As different parts of Sookie, it's significant that Bill and Eric leave her while Tara gains vampire powers and Pam must care for Fangtasia and the vampires' interests in Bon Temps. The feminine in Sookie's life is gaining strength.

Sookie and the Fairies

In her pale blue dress and headband, Sookie resembles Alice in Wonderland when she tumbles into fairyland at the beginning of season four. It's a realm of peace and beauty, everything glowing with light. However, as Sookie abruptly realizes, the beauty covers a wasteland of ugliness and exploitation. Queen Mab is gathering the human-fairy descendants to "harvest" them. The glowing fruit turns rotten in Sookie's eyes and the lovely garden becomes a battlefield of empty cliffs and gaping pits.

The fairies offer Sookie "a lumière—a light fruit" (4.1). Obviously the name means light and they're offering her a symbolic lantern as well as the apple or pomegranate of temptation. Light symbolizes knowledge, and meeting the fairies teaches Sookie the truth of her past, even as she decides who she wants to be in the future. Her Grandpa Earl is sacrificed to get Sookie safely home, and though she discovers a year has passed, she's relieved to have survived her encounter.

This experience also grants her knowledge of her fairy godmother. On the show, Claudine does little, though she protests she's been the one watching over Sookie when she needed it. Symbolically, however, she's determined to protect Sookie from Bill, the predator who's breaking her heart.

When Sookie is comatose after being drained by Bill Compton, Claudine gives her a drink of glowing water and invites her to come "home." Water is a feminine power, an image of healing and life to the dying Sookie. Claudine warns Sookie to not let "him" take her "light" (3.7). In the feminine realm, the liquid sunlight from the life-giving pool is the best thing Sookie has ever tasted. "Don't be fooled. The pond is bigger and deeper than you think," Claudette tells her—the wisdom and magic of the feminine is just as great as that of the patriarchal vampires (3.7). When Bill enters the fairy realm, Claudine blasts him with her power, just as Sookie's friends flung him into the sun. All are determined to protect the heroine at her most vulnerable.

In the books, Claudine saves Sookie from falling asleep at the wheel and wakes her during a house fire. She finally perishes battling to defend her. Further, she leaves Sookie so much money that the desperate waitress can finally become financially independent. As she's described in the books, "Claudine is unpredictable and a lot of fun, though like all fairies, she's dangerous as a tiger when she's angry" (*Dead as a Doornail* 20). Claudine threatens to eat one man, and promises her sister's murderer a four-hour head start before she hunts him for a year. She's a powerful and protective force, before her eventual death.

On the show, Claudine's presence seems more pointless. She protected Sookie as a child but only after her parents were killed. Just after her arrival on earth, Eric drains and kills her, in a scene played for humor rather than pathos. However, her siblings take her place and continue to counsel Sookie. In a fairytale-like plot, Sookie discovers that her ancestor promised his first female heir to a vampire. Also in true fairytale fashion, Sookie's ritual has allowed Warlow to escape banishment and come seeking her.

Maurella, from Andy's forest tryst, is the ultimate mother figure, who's apparently given birth at least 73 other times in her life. Her pregnancy with Andy's child turns out to be four super-accelerated fairies. She's far more powerful than other younger fairies and has a greater knowledge of languages and lore. Since her grandmother's death, Sookie hasn't really had a mother as mentor figure, only sharp-edged, independent Pam and hapless Arlene. Maurella could become that mentor. Surrounded by the women of the bar, Maurella gives birth to many babies. For a moment, she seems to be creating a perfect feminine community of love and protection. However, she soon vanishes. Her surviving child is a mirror for Sookie, another telepathic half-fae who must find power in her life rather than letting Bill exploit her.

With the fairies' aid, Sookie sees through her mother's eyes and gets a look at the vampire that killed her parents. At the same time, she absorbs some of her perspective. Her mother was all Sookie was not—a stable, normal woman who resented the magical and wanted nothing to do with it. As such, she's another shadow for Sookie. Then Sookie's gaze changes to the vampire's. In an original script draft, she sees an image of vampire Sookie. This was replaced with a nasty male face (probably less confusing to the audience) but Sookie in her vision becomes that menace—the wicked force that killed her parents ("First Draft: Vampire Sookie" 5.8). She watches through the vampire's eyes as he kills her mother and then finds the Band-Aid with Sookie's blood in the backseat. As she faces her dark side and sees through its eyes, she learns from the encounter.

"A dark time is coming. You will be tested. Hold onto your light. As long as you can hold onto your light, you will be free," the oldest fairy on earth, the Elder, tells Sookie (5.11). The Elder is scatterbrained and easily distracted—traditionally feminized traits. Thus Sookie finds a "real" female mentor, but one as short-lived and useless as Claudine. Sookie discovers her "light" is finite and tries to use it all up, but Jason reminds her that her powers have brought her occasional happiness by letting her connect with her gran. It seems giving up her magic is not the answer—she'll need it.

In a bright pink dress, Sookie confronts the Elder. She agrees to aid Sookie in her fight, and with an entire clan of fairies behind her, Sookie looks prepared to go to war. However, Russell defeats the Elder and drains her. With the fairy power he's stolen from her, he can see into their invisible stronghold. As Sookie stands there in the front and center, she is their only possible general. She leads them all in blasting Russell, and together with Eric, they kill him. Sookie has grown from supplicant to warrior queen, in time for the greater battle that's coming.

Battling the Patriarchy

The vampires' power structure is hierarchical in a traditional male pattern: Bill reports to Sheriff Eric, who reports to the monarchy, who reports to the Authority, itself a term granted to this kind of power structure. There's Pam the secretary and Jessica the rebellious daughter. There's the vapid queen Sophie-Ann who's easily intimidated by the king and otherwise has little grasp of reality. Compared with this are the males jostling for power: Eric, Bill, Russell Edgington, the dreaded Magister and the Authority. With comments like "she is mine," hierarchy and protocol are everything. At the same time, the system is corrupt, antiquated, and bereft of compassion or occasionally logic. Russell Edgington notes, "The Magister is a nasty little... Anachronistic toad, a ridiculous remnant of the Middle Ages. The only power he has over us is the power we give him" (3.5).

Sookie subverts this by tossing her blonde ponytail and cutting through male posturing with her feminine intuition. She sees that Alcide's pack leader is helpless and afraid beneath his arrogance and reports this fact. She refuses to obey orders and bargains for money and favors in return for Eric's errands. In short, she demands respect and makes sure she gets it. In romance, she's the one calling the shots as she breaks up with both her vampire boyfriends: Sam, Alcide, and others are only waiting for her to choose them to take their places.

When Sookie enters the fairies' club on earth, she's in a feminine utopia, a sexy dark world contrasted with the ethereal paradise of fairyland. Magic symbolically comes from emotion and intuition—classically feminine qualities. When Russell the destroyer kills the Elder, Sookie stands side by side with the other fairies, wielding their feminine "light" to defend their refuge.

The Vampire Authority and the fairies are each what the

other rejects—one technological and powerful with a strict hierarchy, the other loosely-organized, tiny and magical. The vampires have the iStakes, a complex silver-delivery system, and a modern stronghold. They rule unquestioningly with the power of only their name. By contrast, the fairies' dwindling power comes from hiding and letting everyone think they've all died.

On her own show, Buffy fights beside a loosely-organized team of males and female who take turns leading. This is similar to Sookie's allies who meet in her home and make plans to save Bon Temps from the forces of destruction. Both are anti-authoritarian, flexible, and improvisational. Critic Karen Sayer perceives Buffy's circle as a feminine utopia, based on support and cooperation, a "home and family," as opposed to "the fractured, driven, individualized and consequently masculine world of vampires and adults" (112). The male hierarchy is the most famous model in Western civilization—when Buffy rejects her own Watcher's Council, "she is challenging a political philosophy which is more than two thousand years old and championing a feminism which has existed for less than a century" (Playden 128). Sookie is beginning to do the same.

Online, *True Blood* fandom is more than half female, as they expand from the mystery-romance novels to the show. Posting boards offer "a predominantly feminine space in which to share fantasies and exchange opinions about the text." As such, "*True Blood* offers a challenge to the more dominant patriarchal ordering of sexual imagery toward more democratic forms of representation and reception" (Brick 61). The world of *True Blood,* reflecting Sookie's community, has become another feminine sphere.

Meanwhile, the Authority is an authoritative, controlling force that even extends control over the feminine sphere. Salome claims fairies are an abomination while Russell plans to control and kill them, capturing their headquarters and breeding them in order to prey on their children. Both sides of the Authority decide the fairies must be dominated, body and soul.

"The Authority can do whatever they want with you and your body," Pam tells Tara (5.11). Both protest the Authority's determination to tell them when to procreate—the male hierarchy is ruling over the female body. Though Bill is male, he too is forced to procreate and make Jessica as a punishment.

Sookie, subverter of the male power structure, is subjected to several real and metaphorical rapes. In the Fellowship of the Sun's basement, she's nearly raped before Godric rescues her. The maenad Maryann bites her in the woods, penetrating her body, then later invades and defiles her home. When Sookie stakes Lorena and saves Bill from Russell Edgington's house, he loses control and feeds on her, nearly to the point of death as she struggles and protests. In the book, this is an actual rape scene as he has nonconsensual sex with her as well as feeding off her. As she struggles to preserve fairykind from the same attacks, she is threatened in her body as well as her life.

In *All Together Dead*, Sophie-Ann's male assistant insists that Sookie exchange blood with him to better serve the queen. Before he can force her, Eric offers to create the bond himself. It's a sexual, uncomfortable feeding, as Sookie loathes doing it, and Eric takes much pleasure from the encounter, forced on them both as it is. Season six has a similar scene, when Sarah Newlin forces Jessica into the vampire camp's "copulation study." Her partner James insists, "I'm a vampire, not a rapist," but when he's put to torture, Jessica volunteers. James still refuses.

> James: You're a beautiful person and you don't deserve this.
> Jessica: I'm not a person. You have to. (6.6)

Despite their dehumanizing prison, a product of the US government, James keeps his humanity and insists Jessica keep hers.

Likewise, in season six, Bill breaks into Sookie's house and decides to drag her away by force and synthesize her blood. He immobilizes Jason, grabs Sookie, and would carry out his threat except that he's moved by Sookie's emotional plea and relents. This too is a metaphorical near-rape as he wants to penetrate her body and take her blood without her consent.

In season five, the Authority dismisses the General's threats of terrible weapons, which are later used on the new vampire Tara, often the victim of the series. Now vampire and homosexual as well as black and female, she's probably the most marginalized character of the story. "It seems telling that *True Blood's* victims are, so often, female or homosexual or nonwhite" (Waters 43). Lafayette is tortured by Eric, Jason's conquests Maudette, Dawn, and Amy die, and various victims include the prostitutes and male-on-male blood donors Janella, Jerry, Destiny, and Tony. Jesus is killed in Marnie's power struggle. Luna dies defending her daughter, and Emma is repeatedly kidnapped. Sookie and her friends like Sam become the only possible protectors of the underprivileged, while the patriarchy seeks to destroy them.

By season five, Bill is no longer king, but a rebel against the system like Eric. This is a more traditional role for vampires— the defiers of the system, not the creators of it. The Authority itself is a patriarchal castle like the Church of the Sun or Fangtasia with Eric on his throne, but underground, the place of Initiation. To save loved ones, most characters descend into the Council in season five, from Pam and Tara to Sam and Luna to Sookie and Jason.

Roman Zjimojic (played by Christopher Meloni) is the Authority's undisputed ruler, the stern voice that's been directing events since the Great Revelation, the power behind the Magister, Nan Flanagan, and the kings.

> "He's a vampire wanting to change the system, fighting against what he sees as fanatics. He's a man interested in co-existence. I think he's a forward-thinking guy," says Meloni, "this supreme example of a man of authority, and yet there are certain moments of him that are surprisingly childish." (Keveney, "'True Blood' Sinks its Teeth")

At the same time, his paranoia and despotism leads to his murder. His enemy Russell is the force of total bloodthirstiness—Roman reveals to Eric and Bill that Russell has become a "poster boy" for Sanguinistas for what he did on public television. "Russell is a pretty powerful vampire. He really represents chaos and anarchy. That is the one thing that my character just disdains, both personally and professionally," Meloni adds (Keveney, "'True Blood' Sinks its Teeth"). In this dualistic government, Roman and his ancient followers die, clearing the way for a new voice...Salome's.

At over 2000, Salome Agrippa is the Guardian of the Authority. In the Bible, Salome was famous for her dance of the seven veils, which won her a murder as reward. The passage states:

> When Herod's birthday was kept, the daughter of Herodias danced before them, and pleased Herod. Whereupon he promised with an oath to give her whatsoever she would ask. And she, being before instructed of her mother, said, "Give me here John Baptist's head in a charger." And the king was sorry: nevertheless for the oath's sake, and them which sat with him at meat, he commanded it to be given her. And he sent, and beheaded John in the prison. And his head was brought in a charger, and given to the damsel: and she brought it to her mother (Matthew 14:6-11).

On the show, her history is related to be somewhat different—her mother sold her virginity to Herod in return for the murder. Salome Agrippa's actress Valentina Cervi relates, "She has a big wound—she's been betrayed when she was a kid...the seductress thing is something that keeps her safe. But there's a whole other world underneath." ("The Real Salome")

The reason for her name soon become apparent: Salome, the Bible's most famous seductress, seduces everyone around her, from the Authority's leader Roman Zjimojic to Bill. Though she's one of the most powerful vampires alive, she doesn't act directly, instead enlisting Russell Edgington to commit Zjimojic's murder. In a masculine world, sex becomes her fast track to power.

In the gender wars she is disturbing—her immense age hasn't brought her enlightenment as it did Godric and Zjimojic. Instead, she sees humans as nothing but food, and she institutes a policy of death. "Vampires shall rightfully rule this earth," she cries like a true fanatic (5.12).

This may well be how the rhetoric of the Religious Right appears to some Americans, particularly those who are not familiar with Biblical literature. For young Americans raised in secular households, the claim that marriage rights cannot be extended to gay couples because of passages found in Leviticus is likely just as unfathomable (if not repugnant) as Agrippa's claim that humans are food because it is written in the Book of Lilith. (Laycock)

In her dealings with Lilith, she's gullible and surprisingly assured of her destiny, a certainty that gets her killed. She even falls for Bill's classic reverse psychology. After Russell slaps her across the room, she doesn't fight back. When Russell flouts her authority and walks out, there's nothing she can do. Throughout her arc, she remains an example, like Sophie-Ann, of the ineffectual feminine leader. With her fanatical last words she compliments Bill for outwitting and destroying her.

"Billith" could become the new vampire Authority with his powers, but he seems to be on a mission more like the coven of season four—total dominance over the opposition and protection for his own people. The new enemy is a stronger patriarchy—the US government and its anti-vampire campaign, led by Louisiana Governor Truman Burrell. However, as he battles the enemy, he becomes it.

Both patriarchies pride themselves on technology, from the Authority's iStakes to the US government's UV bullets. The US government and Authority have immense budgets, unlimited troops, the force of law. Sadly, they use modern rationality and science to create obscene weapons of suffering and control—the liquid silver delivery system, overhead UV radiation, surveillance. By dehumanizing and experimenting on innocents outside their control, the governmental institutions set themselves up as the monsters. Governor Burrell condemns vampires to a "camp" where they are physically and psychologically tortured. He intends "The extinction of your race," as he tells Bill (6.6). This echoes concentration camps throughout history where political dissident and marginalized "races" were disposed of. (In fact, human beings are genetically all the same race, so this is a misnomer.) "The best scapegoats are peripheral members of the community who lack the sort of status or connections that would protect them from persecution" (Corn and Dunn 150). It's a short road from resentment to hatred to genocide.

> "We wanted to play with the politics/religion angle, since that seems to be something that never stops," creator Alan Ball says. "Some of the things being said by some people during the Republican primary were so horrifying to me that I thought, 'What if vampires wanted a theocracy? What would that look like?' Whenever anybody thinks they know what God wants and wants to apply that to government, whether Americans or the Taliban, it's kind of a terrifying thing." (Keveney, "'True Blood' Sinks its Teeth")

The few vampires and sympathetic humans of Eric's "Area Five" cannot stand against them physically…they must resort to trickery to keep their small community alive. Kristin Bauer van Straten (Pam) explains that she and her friends have "only has a couple options—go underground or fight back. We definitely see how all the vampires react under pressure" (Halterman).

Guarded by rapists and murderers, Tara counsels Willa to get past their contact lenses and glamour the guards. This she does, sweetly requesting a word in private with a guard, who eagerly agrees. The marginalized gender and species is striking back.

They win in the end by feeding on Bill, who offers his body in a gesture of total self-sacrifice. Eric, busy ripping off arms and dealing out punishments, is taking the more macho approach. However, he and Jason only arrive in time to watch Bill save their loved ones.

As the series jumps ahead six months, the world has changed into the "new age" described in the song "Radioactive" for which the final episode of season six is named.

The government is gone with no national or state support. "This town, Bon Temps, we're on our own," Sam says (6.10). As the new mayor, he's a voice of support for those who are marginalized—the antiestablishment is in power now. When they meet in a church (a place of hope, healing, and kindness—

the feminized authority), he reveals his plan, not for strict government in the crisis, but for a new world of partnerships and trust. "If we're gonna be safe, every single human needs a vampire, and every vampire needs a human," Sam tells them (6.10). Brian Buckner explains:

> I feel like this show is ultimately about the relationship between vampires and humans and it's about this town. I want to bring it in a little bit. I feel like at times we've hurt ourselves...My goal is to get all these people living under the umbrella of one story and one threat ... and make it about this small town we've all come to know and love. (Keveney, "HBO's 'True Blood' Going Back")

Hepatitis V is said to create a new era of "togetherness"— with tainted TruBlood and tainted vampires, the humans and vampires of Bon Temps must rely on each other to survive. This brings a chance to make amends for Lettie Mae and Jessica, and possibly for Bill and Sookie to begin a new understanding. The "strange and unprecedented times" may put an end to the vampire-human hostility and create a new kind of community, a small town bound together in support of one another—a feminized community of partnership rather than the hierarchy of governor or Authority.

Niall, Warlow, and the Truth Revealed

The sixth season introduces a stronger mentor, as Sookie's great-grandfather Niall, a fairy king, returns from exile to aid them. With teleportation, powerful blasts of light, and visions of the past and future, he's the toughest fairy seen yet. He's also an incredible source of information. "There is a power within the fae of our bloodline. A secret that has been passed down for generations," he reveals (6.2). In the books, he's leading half of a fairy civil war (the other side considers mixed bloods like Sookie abominations). On the show, he tests Jason (and notes that Jason failed). And he teaches Sookie to use her light as a devastating final strike, warning that she will lose all her abilities if she uses it. As he instructs her to "Pour in all your love, all your pain, all your secrets and hopes, dreams," he's urging her to focus her emotions, the feelings she's been nurturing for her community, but turned outwards.

"It's like the sun," Sookie whispers (6.2). It's not surprising that this daylight child's power is a ball of light.

Like Claudine, Niall is a master of dimensional travel, secure in the fairy world and the human one. This is another skill Sookie must master, both to banish Warlow and to gain comfort with her mysterious fairy nature.

This mentor, a parent figure who dismisses their weak powers and inexperience, is benevolent and cruel, following Jason's visions of his parents' dark sides, as they urge him to kill vampires. As Sookie thinks, "He put his arms around me and I felt his incredible beauty, his terrifying magic, and his crazy devotion. There was nothing human about him" (*Deadlocked* 305). This foreshadows revelations about their parents, as Sookie reveals their parents didn't know how to handle her.

"For a mother [or father] to happily raise a child who is slightly or largely different in psyche and soul needs from that of the mainstream culture, she must have a start on some heroic qualities herself to stand up for her child and for what she believes" (Estés 176). Some fantasy stories feature "super-parents," like Clark Kent's parents, who know about his abilities and supportively help him train them. However, most parents in fantasy are more like the obstructive aunt and uncle who adopt Harry Potter, or Katniss's useless burden of a mother.

Many parents do their best to bury or reject their children's magical powers and encourage them to be "normal." Estés notes, "A woman in such an environ will often try to mold her daughter so she acts 'properly' in the outside world" (175). Sookie's parents failed the test—upon discovering Warlow intended to make Sookie a vampire-fairy like himself, they planned her death.

The name Warlow echoes Marlow, the vampire in *30 Days of Night*. Likewise, Stephen King's *Salem's Lot* speculates on what would happen if a vampire descended on an American small town. The story focuses on the town dwellers' hope and fears until the vampire hunters finally confront Master Vampire Barlow.

Sookie has defeated vampires with sunlight and stakes, but Warlow is a vampire-fairy—all her gifts and all her opponents' gifts as well. Nora reveals that Warlow, like Sookie, is something unique. According to her new translation, he is the only one who can make Lilith meet the sun, because he is her progeny (6.4). In fact, he echoes Sookie in many ways. "I've had a lot of bad in my life—I was hoping for a little slice of something good," he reveals. Sookie has said the same about herself. When Sookie hesitates to accept his dinner offer, his sensitivity lets him cut through her excuses to ask, "Who's Bill?" (6.2).

Warlow is an enemy, but also strangely an ally, as like Eric and Bill, he's devoted to Sookie and would do anything to be with her. "I am coming for you! You are mine!" he tells her, echoing her vampire lovers (5.8). He killed her parents, but as he reveals, he did it to save her and he's drawn to her as she was to the vampires. "The darkness in me; it battles with the light every second of my being," Warlow says (6.4). This enemy-ally, caught between light and dark, represents another shadow for Sookie. She too is a fairy tied to the vampires, deciding which side she will take in the growing conflict. As Warlow channels the photokinesis said to be a secret of Sookie's family, they share a mysterious connection. He enters Sookie's life by lying and charming. To defeat him, Sookie takes the same path, dosing his food with silver, asking him on a date, and even halfway seducing him. To match his lies, she becomes a liar herself.

He's also a shadow for "Bilith" as his destined foe and son. Both are obsessed with Sookie, and Warlow and Lilith are the two oldest vampires in existence—the vampire war will turn on their actions. Both have extraordinary vampire powers, including blood with unique vampire power. "Sookie is a faerie, her blood is royal as is mine. It's been passed down through our line for millennia," Warlow notes (6.5). Warlow can walk in the sun, which as Bill reveals, is his new craving and destiny as he attempts to recreate fairy blood with science.

Sookie banishes her father from her presence and thanks Warlow for saving her. "She's confronted her father finally, and her relationship with Warlow is deepening," director Howard Deutch explains. Warlow pleads for acceptance, touching her in a way needy innocent Eric once did:

> I killed Lillith because I despise what she's turned me into. I despise the pain, the aching hunger inside me. I despise what this hunger has made me do, but if you agreed to be mine, it would all be over, it would be a closed circle, you and me. We could live wherever want, go wherever we want we could be everything to each other because we would need only one another's blood to survive. I would never have to hurt anybody else. There would never be anybody else, just you and me. (6.6)

Sookie, drawn to Warlow in a way "she can't stop feeling," saves him from Bill by taking him to fairyland. There in the Edenic garden, she ties him up, and, in a very self-directed moment, seduces him and gives into her feelings. "Sookie has really matured. It's really a self-aware Sookie, Sookie with a self-knowledge that we've never seen before," comments Daniel Kenneth, the episode's writer. Anna Paquin adds:

> She's not being anyone's doormat. She's sick of taking whatever from whomever. She's more independent, strong and tough. I feel like she's actually finally learning from all the incredibly, odd, bizarre and unfortunate stuff that's happened to her. (Keveney, "HBO's 'True Blood' Going Back")

As Nora reads in the Vampire Bible, "And so it was that the people led Lilith to the sun, and so it shall be again. As the blood ascends, two will become one. When light and dark collide, our salvation is at hand" (6.2). With the final battle approaching, Sookie struggles to master her feelings and choose a side, which will define the new world she creates.

However, when she tries to bring Warlow into her world and make him part of her life, he reveals himself as another predator. The situation seems terribly cliché as Warlow demands his eternal bride and threatens to wed her by force.

> Warlow: In a thousand, two thousand years, you'll learn to love me.
> Sookie: I don't think so! (6.10)

The powerful heroine becomes a classic gothic maiden, tied to a tree and screaming for help from the vicious predator, then saved by her menfolk. As Sookie prepares to use or sacrifice her light (and never does), Bill, Jason, Andy, Adelaine, and even Niall arrive at the last moments to save her.

While Jason takes revenge on the monster that killed his family, Sookie manages only to hide in the shower and shriek. Her empowerment fades away and she finds herself wanting an ordinary relationship with Alcide, a (somewhat) ordinary guy, far from the world of vampires and fairies.

However, she isn't done with the magical world of night and the supernatural. Bill confronts her when she refuses to donate blood to a vampire, saying, "You need a vampire in your life, Sookie. Moreso than anyone else here. You need protection" (6.10). As the infected vampires attack, Sookie will need to choose the path her life will take and the man she chooses to share it.

BLOODSUCKERS ON THE BAYOU

Other Characters' Classic Journeys

The books are told from Sookie's point of view, and characters there mirror her even more than on the show—when she's happy her friends get married and settle down. When she's miserable, they go through breakups. No one has lengthy adventures in the Vampire Authority or among the werewolves unless she comes along.

On *True Blood,* however, characters in the later seasons have strong arcs. There are major plotlines Sookie never sees that change her friends forever—in fact, some of her friends undergo hero's and heroine's journeys as they too face their shadow selves and descend into death, only to reemerge stronger.

Love in Bon Temps

Romance is problematic on the show. "Bon Temps is full of people who ache to share themselves deeply with someone, but when they try to do so, the result is often a bloodbath. Ball wisely takes a playful, ironic approach to these dark themes, and by doing so leaves some room for hope, however irrational it may seem" (Poole 87).

Bad relationships fill Bon Temps. Some are abusive and filled with dangerous secrets and treacheries: René and Arlene, Eggs and Tara, Franklin and Tara, Sam and Daphne, Alcide and Debbie, Sookie and Warlow. Others are destructive and hurt others: Jason's many shallow flings, including his relationship with Jessica and affair with Sarah Newlin. Bill's incestuous affair with Portia. Lettie Mae's relationship with the cheating pastor. Salome uses sex as a weapon, much like Lorena, and all their affairs are destructive. Russell and Talbot genuinely love each other, but when Talbot is killed, Russell goes on an insane violent rampage. After two bad relationships with Bill and Eric (there were good moments, but the men are ultimately vampires, and thus self-serving and often a threat to Sookie), Sookie finds herself intrigued by Warlow, the latest in a series of predators and users. He ends up being even more savage than Eric or Bill and Sookie flees to Alcide's normalcy.

In the books, characters like Sam and Jason (and Sookie!) go through many destructive relationships. By the final book, all are prepared to settle down with someone stable who can improve their lives rather than these catastrophic violent relationships full of angst and drama.

The only good relationships that appear to last are Andy and Holly's (albeit with a few snags) and Arlene and Terry's (until recent events). These characters, despite Holly's wiccan training, are the most ordinarily human on the show. By contrast, Hoyt and Jessica's relationship, like Tara's with her season four girlfriend Naomi, fell apart because the love was unequal and a craving for danger and magic intruded into the prosaic relationship.

At the same time, several relationships guide the human member into a higher plane of spirituality or magic. This is the effect Bill has on Sookie, Jesus has on Lafayette, Luna has on Sam, Crystal has on Jason. Andy's brief affair with the fairy Maurella has on him. (In fact, Maurella, Luna, and Crystal also bring their men families to look after as a way of grounding them and forcing them to grow up). Most of these relationships begin in the woods, the dark unconscious world. However, all these romantic figures soon leave the picture, leaving the main character sadder but wiser as he or she grows toward a deeper understanding.

It's left to be seen which category Pam and Tara will fall into in season seven. "[Vampires are] in a bit of crisis this year, so the vampire relationships are developing and being challenged under fire. There isn't a ton of time for romance,"

Kristin Bauer van Straten noted in season six (Mullins).

The larger question (addressed with the release of Harris's final novel) is whom Sookie will end up with. Harris said of Sookie's experience, "I think she's learned something from all the relationships she's had, from starting out as a young woman who had never had a serious relationship or a satiable relationship, she's compressed a lot of experience into the last few years" (Tyley, "True Blood Books"). It's certainly notable that in books and show, every male character appears hopelessly in love with her, to the disgust of characters like Pam, who can't understand the men's obsession.

Of course, this is Sookie's story, and love triangles are a popular trope. Relationship expert Gilda Carle explains:

> We want to be fought over. It makes us feel more like a prize. And a suitor wants to fight over us, so he feels he has won a prize, something not so easily gotten. In real life, triangles are horrible. But by vicariously enjoying them in books and movies, we can deal with them more appropriately. (Wloszczyna 1)

There are many love triangles (or more complex patterns) in the series: Summer-Hoyt-Jessica-Tommy, then Hoyt-Jessica-Jason. Rene-Arlene-Terry. Debbie-Alcide-Sookie. James-Jessica-Jason-Violet. Most famously, Sookie is torn between Bill and Eric, but Alcide, Sam, and others take an interest, including (in the book series) Crystal's were-panther uncle Calvin Norris and Quinn the weretiger. Sam or Alcide represents a normal life with children, daylight, and a shared business, while the vampires offer a more subversive, nontraditional relationship. Of course, Sookie has the power here, as she's the one to make all the romantic choices while the men hang back hopefully. "Why limit it to just Bill and Eric?" Charlaine Harris laughs. "It could be neither, it could be nobody!" (Tyley "True Blood Books").

Family

The concept of family, birth and chosen, is essential to the series. Sookie's parents feared her and Tara's mother abused her. Both of Sam's families abused him as well, and Tommy's parents turned him into an awful person. Jessica's father beat her. Pam's parents apparently sent her away for being attracted to women. Lafayette's mother disowned him for his life choices, but he spends all his money maintaining her. Only the brother-sister pairing of Sookie and Jason or cousins like Tara and Lafayette or Andy and Terry are shown to be positive birth family relationships.

Contrasted with these are the supernatural "adoptive" families. Eric sincerely mourns Godric, though Bill and Lorena's relationship was filled with misery. By the fifth and sixth seasons, Jessica and Bill appear devoted to each other, as she resolves to stay with "Bilith" no matter what he becomes. Jessica's actress Deborah Ann Woll reflects on "Parent and child obviously even being even more connected than…with a girlfriend or a wife or husband… [Bill] will always be Jessica's maker. And with a vampire, that can go on through eternity."

Eric explains to Pam, "Becoming a Maker is an eternal commitment. Greater than any marriage, deeper than any human bond" (5.3). He calls abandoning progeny a "sacrilege." One assumes he learned this from Godric, who likely treated his progeny honorably and lovingly. After remembering Eric's speech, Pam vows to do the same for her progeny, Tara, and offers her life for her several times as well as giving her a home and job. Eric in turn has only sired two progeny. He creates Willa as a tool against her father, but assures her she's important to him. He's genuinely revolted when he hears her father rejected her and sent her to the vampire concentration camp.

The werewolf pack, another adoptive family relationship, is shown as sacred to Alcide, from his memorable adolescent initiation, in which he proclaimed, "I choose pack," to his risking his life to save the pack from addiction to V. He kidnaps Emma repeatedly because she's a werewolf and he feels she should be raised with her own kind. Sam, likewise vows to protect his adopted daughter Emma, as Terry does for Arlene's children, even her son by René.

Bill

Bill is on a quest for belonging in season one as he attempts to settle into his family home and falls for Sookie. The next season, his family life gets more complicated as he gets a teenage daughter and then his maker returns for him. Season three, he's entangled in vampire politics as Sookie and Lorena, the good girl and the bad girl, fight for his loyalty. He lets Sookie go from a desire to protect her, and the many secrets he's kept from her blow up between them. The first four seasons, even as he becomes king, most of his scenes revolve around Sookie and their shared enemies. In season five, both Eric and Bill drink Lilith's blood and descend into their shadow sides, mindlessly feeding on humans. But as they also enter the Authority, they've begun their own quest in the world of vampires.

Bill follows the rules no matter what—vampire law, human law—it doesn't matter. Thus he recycles but also accepts his vampire punishment and turns Jessica. When Lilith returns, he's seen mindlessly following her laws—when Salome tells him, "To refuse God's gift to us is blasphemy," Bill obeys and feeds on a tearful human (5.8). After, he reveals the secret to destroying mainstreamers—destroy TruBlood, the one thing that has allowed mainstreaming. As one of them, Bill knows how to bring them down. He explains that he's "evolving" but when he suggests vampires be forced to feed on humans "as they were meant to" he's just trading one rulebook for another (5.8).

The new believer Bill voices feelings that he's kept unexpressed for years. His new mindset allows him to loathe humans and stop pandering to them: "They used to drive me crazy—worrying about their feelings and their mortality and their weakness," he says (5.11). Giving himself over to Lilith's cult is a relief for him. "I have spent my entire life as a vampire apologizing, believing I was inherently wrong somehow. Living in fear. Fear that God had forsaken me. That I was damned. But Lilith grants us freedom from fear," Bill tells Sookie (5.12).

At the same time, part of him is floundering. As he has sex with Salome, he sees her as Sookie, the positive Anima, and Lilith, the negative one. Season six sees him begging Lilith for direction in his life. He's on a true believer's mission to save his fellow vampires from Governor Burrell's contaminated TruBlood and protect his race, but he's also filled with greed and loathing for Warlow, who has vampire-fairy blood and soon has Sookie.

He puts himself in a near-coma to seek Lilith's counsel, and finds himself having visions of a vampire mass-execution across the world. He, as Lilith's chosen, is their only possible defender. "William Compton, it is all on you. The time to act is now. Do not come to me seeking answers again," she says (6.6). Unable to synthesize Warlow's blood through science, he takes a leap of faith and drinks it.

He tries to get Warlow's blood for himself, but Eric has taken it first and Sookie turns him away angrily. In the vampire camp, Bill allows all his friends to feed off him and falls into near-death, saving his friends with his blood in a true messianic moment. He revives thanks to Jessica's love and leaves with his friends, having saved vampirekind.

His strictness and inflexibility makes him hesitate rather than save Sookie from Warlow, because he's treated her badly in the past. True justice would mean there's no chance of forgiveness. However, Jessica, voice of his humanity, convinces him to save her, which he does at the risk of his life. Though his love theme for Sookie plays, his feelings for her are voiced in terms of protection and responsibility rather than passion.

Six months later, he commits, not to Sookie, but to the truth, revealing the origins of Hepatitis V in his book *And God Bled* in order, as he says, "To establish trust. To end all the secrets" (6.10). Though he admits to murdering Governor Burrell, he relies on pure justice to protect him, pointing out "It's not like he didn't deserve it" and "what jury would convict me" (6.10). His ordeal with Lilith changed his actions, but not his fundamental personality.

Eric

Eric of course is the trickster of the story. His major tricks involve persuading Russell to try daywalking and Sookie to drink his blood and suck a bullet out of him. His daywalking trick gets him everything he wants, including an intricate, painful revenge on Russell and also a chance to feed off Sookie without consequences.

"You weren't there on that roof with Godric. I saw a whole other side to him, and it was real," Sookie tells Bill (3.11). Among his whims and selfishness, family loyalty is indeed sacred to Eric, not only loyalty toward Godric and Pam, but also to his slaughtered human family. Eric faces the patriarchy and family responsibility together when he takes on Russell, his sworn king and killer of his human father. He is the establishment, and Eric, subverter of the establishment. Nonetheless, Eric literally chains them together in the daylight so they can die together. As they die, however, Eric has a vision of Godric counseling mercy and love. He cannot bear to turn back from his quest of vengeance, but his friend Sookie, who often represents his conscience, saves Russell for him. Eric and Bill finally unite to bury Russell in concrete. Though Godric protests in Eric's head, Eric ends season three unable to accept Godric's plea for tolerance.

In season four, Eric turns into shadows of himself—a complete innocent with no barriers to loving Sookie, a dream Eric willing to share her with Bill, and a mind-controlled slave on a mission to execute Bill. As these shadows, Eric can fulfill all his deepest fantasies: He can faultlessly murder Bill, win over Sookie, have it all. Eric dreams Godric appears and goads him to devour Sookie, taunting him than he's incapable of love however, as Eric confesses in his dream, he hopes Sookie can redeem him.

Eric's nemesis is Russell Edgington, especially when Russell takes over the Authority and Eric's determined to rebel against them. Season five introduces his sister Nora. They call each other "brother" and "sister" during sex and "fight like siblings," adding another layer of disturbing incest to the relationship (5.1). However, Eric is horrified by his sister's fundamentalist attitude. While he remains anti-authoritarian, he sets out on a personal mission to redeem her. In season five, he becomes a master manipulator, working his way through fundamentalist vampires to save his sister and himself. He apologizes to Russell and kisses his ring even as he plots the Sanguinistas' destruction.

In season six, he walks into the concentration camp to rescue Pam. There he faces Governor Burrell, the enemy of all he stands for, who kills Nora to torture him. "I want my daughter back, I want you to feel the same immeasurable loss, I want you to understand what it's like to lose a part of who you are," he says (6.6). There in the darkest place of all, Eric faces death—that of the woman he loves rather than his own. Nora's suffering inspires his crafty escape but also his change of faith.

He goes to Bill and for the first time, says he believes in the teachings of Lilith: "I don't know what you are, all I know is I saw Sookie stake you and you survived but if you are God...please heal her for me" (6.7). Eric humbles himself in a way he's only done with his maker. Bill is the establishment and faith together, but Bill has the power he needs. "You want me to say the words? I believe you, I believe in you. I believe you are divine," Eric pleads (6.7). Alas, faith is not enough, and Eric loses Nora. He charges into the vampire camp and saves all his loved ones (and Jason) but goes off to heal his wounds...before he finds himself meeting the sun in a compelling cliffhanger.

Bill vs Eric

"From his preternatural calm to his gravelly voice and command of multiple languages, Eric is the anti-Bill. I'm not sure anyone considered Swedish to be sexy, but we learn something new every day, now, don't we?" (Rubin 27). Indeed, Eric was designed to be an anti-Bill. "In many ways, Eric is Bill's opposite, absolutely on purpose," the author confirmed. He's based somewhat on *The Thirteenth Warrior* in contrast to Bill, the Southern gentleman ("Charlaine Harris Answers Questions from her Fans" 309).

Bill wants to mainstream—live in Bon Temps and fit in with humanity. Old people get along well with him, as Sookie's and Andy's grandmothers both recall a time when Southern gentlemen practiced Southern charm and courtly behavior. Bill even rides a horse at one point and fantasizes about Sookie in layers of petticoats. He chooses to fix up the old Compton place rather than create a new home for himself and sometimes sleeps in the town graveyard. He's clinging to his human past and fighting to be a part of Bon Temps—the harmless old vampire living near the old Stackhouse place.

Eric, by contrast, has set himself up as a tourist attraction—the vampire lord of Fangtasia, dominating from a throne. His bar is a place for hot young people, fangbangers and wannabe vampires all in slinky black. He has the coolest cars, the newest tech. Though he's older than Eric, he's a vampire of the future, while Bill as a relic of his time.

As the fourth season begins, however, Eric and Bill switch roles. Eric, on camera before the American public, is trying to minimize differences. As he puts it, "I'm a tax-paying American and small business owner in the great state of Louisiana. I also happen to be a vampire" (4.1). He reminds viewers that as a vampire, he's more trustworthy than a politician.

Meanwhile, the scene cuts to Bill, now a well-dressed politician at a ribbon-cutting. Bill has become the King of Louisiana and now acts like the town's aristocracy, rather than an ordinary citizen. He's also emphasizing his other differences, as he reminds everyone he's the "oldest member of the community" (4.1). "All of your subjects are learning how ruthless you are," Pam tells Bill (4.4). She later calls him a "self-loathing, power-hungry, pompous little dork" (4.6). He's turned distant and controlled enough to finally kill Marnie with a gun, not his fangs.

Jealous over Sookie and filled with hatred for Eric, Bill coldly arranges his execution and only stops himself when Eric confesses that he was a barbarian who doesn't deserve mercy and hopes Bill will give Sookie a chance for happiness. Hearing that innocent voice saying what Bill once said—that he came alive when he met Sookie and that her happiness is all that matters, Bill relents and frees Eric. Despite their differences, their similarities often hit home for one or the other, especially their overwhelming feelings for Sookie.

> Bill: Look what he did to you. He's betrayed you, used you, drawn you into danger. [Sookie looks at him.] Yes, I've made mistakes trying to keep you safe, but I'm nothing like Eric. (3.11)

In fact, he is.

Despite Eric's role as sheriff, he seems determined to destroy the status quo rather than maintain it—as a force of chaos, he is the anti-authority, driven by whim, impulse, and affection rather than the strict rules that drive Bill. "Eric will never be a king unless he can control himself better," Pam notes (*All Together Dead* 87). Bill's control is everything to him.

The pair act like shadows for each other, reminding each other of flaws and constantly goading. "So you would sacrifice my progeny but not your own. How very un-kingly of you," Eric tells Bill (4.12). Each says the things the other can't bear to hear.

> "My Sookie hid a corpse?"
> "I don't think you can be too sure about that possessive pronoun."
> "Where did you learn that term, Northman?"
> "I took 'English as a Second Language' at a community college in the seventies.
> Bill said, "She is mine."
> I wondered if my hands would move. They would. I raised both of them, making an unmistakable one-fingered gesture.
> Eric laughed, and Bill said, "Sookie!" in shocked astonishment.
> "I think that Sookie is telling us she belongs to herself," Eric said softly. (*Club Dead* 269)

At season four's end, Bill and Eric unite at last, offering their lives to save Sookie when Marnie demands they kill themselves to save her. After, Sookie breaks up with both of them but they remain united, with Eric standing beside his king and helping him to kill Nan. In season five, they become partners, working together to infiltrate the Authority and remain alive. Alexander Skarsgard (Eric) notes:

> Steve [Moyer] is a really close friend of mine, and I really enjoy the bromance. Eric hated Bill. He thought Bill was insignificant, a young, naïve vampire. Suddenly, he's in a position where he cares about this guy. He protects him

and saves him. That's definitely something new for Eric.
(Keveney, "'True Blood' Sinks its Teeth")

However, both temporarily declare loyalty to the Sanguinistas when they taste the blood of Lilith. Eric has a vision of Godric that snaps him out of it. However, Bill never had a saintly paternal mentor, only the cruel Lorena. Further, he is less flexible and adaptable. While Eric continues undermining the system, Bill becomes Lilith's top disciple and plants himself at the top of the new hierarchy. Once again, they're pitted against each other, though their goals of protecting vampires remain the same.

Sam
Sam the werecollie is a herding dog, in a reflection of his protective role as the employer at his bar. Like a dog, Sam is honest, fair, affectionate, and open-minded. In western art dogs symbolize fidelity, as Sam shows to Sookie and his adoptive family (Shepherd 194).

Sam of course is on a quest to accept himself. He had a horrible youth with the callous Merlottes turning him out at age fifteen, leaving him to wander and discover who he is. He then meets Maryann, who seduces him in his first sexual experience but really just plans to use him for his powers. Later, Sam turns thief and his girlfriend betrays him.

By the time he comes to Bon Temps, he's much more cautious. It's revealed in season one that he's never told anyone about his powers. Only when Sam lets down his guard in his sleep does he reveal to Sookie who he really is. When he does, Sookie is angry at first, but quickly accepts him. Her support helps Sam understand that his shapeshifting can be a positive force in his life. At the end of season one, a drugged-out Sookie lets his powers slip to their friends. Though they laugh it off, Sam feels Sookie's pressure to reveal his secret. "Sam, you need to let people see the real you. 'Cause you're kind and brave. There's nothin' there not to love," she tells him (1.12).

In his relationship with Sookie, Sam is presented as the nice-guy best friend and runner up. Their single date ends awkwardly and is not repeated. He finds consolation with Tara, but she sneaks off before daybreak and is determined to keep him distant.

As one critic notes, "Season one slowly reveals Sam's dark secret and lonely history, but it is in the following two seasons that the viewer begins to learn how dark Sam's history, like his temper, has been" (Mukherjea 118). In season two, Sam meets Daphne Landry, his first shifter. She seeks him out and tells him the truth—he has denied his background for so long that it has come to him. As they begin an affair, he starts believing he could truly be accepted by his own kind as well as outsiders. It's his first step to reaching out to the shifter community—his origin, family, and home. She is a pig, an animal sacred to the Goddess and a symbol of the Otherworld (Walker 385). In the woods, she's nearly torn to pieces, foreshadowing the violence of Maryann the Maenad. After Daphne betrays him, her body is found in Sam's walk-in refrigerator at Merlotte's, with her heart removed. Sam is not only being framed for her murder, he is confronted with her heartless body, reminding him that he too has a piece missing—love, acceptance, and family. Following this, Sam uses his powers to confront the Maenad who first set him on his path. woods

> In season two, however, Sam really came into his own. From growing comfortable in his own skin through an ill-fated dalliance with a fellow shifter, to repeatedly putting his own life on the line to protect the integrity of the town he loves, Sam Merlotte became one stand-up hunk of a dog—err, man. The plaid shirts, cowboy boots, and Texas-sized belt buckles only added to his allure. (Rubin 26)

By revealing his powers to his allies, trusting them to save his life, and battling Maryann rather than hiding from her, Sam saves the town, his community. Sam's journey for the season is coming to grips with what he is and stopping denying it. The one thing he learned from Daphne is that. "It took me this long to realize it, but you suffer a lot hiding something than you do if you face up to it," Sam tells Bill after defeating Maryann (2.12). With these words, he goes questing for his birth family.

Of course, he finds that they're no-good, exploitative country bumpkins—shifty as well as shifters. They also have a family member Sam hadn't expected—a younger brother who enacts his own shadow. Each automatically envies the other— the one with Shifter parents, the other with wealthy parents. Tommy is a pit bull, an animal that's slang for a sharp temper. Further, he challenges Sam's right to belong to the Mickens family, just as Sam's inner voice is doing. However, when Tommy is in trouble, Sam disguises himself as a pit bull like his brother, descends into his brother's dog pits, and confronts his parents.

> Sam: Don't talk to me that way. Like making people scared? Think you're good at it? I can't understand the power you got over them, because I see you for what you are. You're just a scared man in saggy underpants with no discernible life skills whatsoever. Come on, Tommy.
> Melinda: Where are you going?
> Sam: Taking him with me…Come on, Tommy. You coming with me? Tommy, I can't promise you a perfect life, but I can promise you it'll be better than this one.
> Tommy: Yeah, I'm coming. (3.7)

Thus Sam rescues his younger brother and tries to convince him of his potential. To Sam, Tommy is the lost childlike part of himself who could have a better life than he does. However, as Tommy goes down bad paths, stealing and choosing violence over good behavior, Sam dreams of his own troubled past as a thief and occasional killer and lashes out at the people around him. Tommy has scars on the outside, as Sam has emotional scars from constant rejection.

> Tommy: You pick it up! Look at yourself. Drunk and yelling. You're nothing but Joe Lee in a Sam suit.
> Sam: You ungrateful little punk. All I've done is help you, and all you've done's been a whiny-ass bitch! I'm through with you! You're fired! Pack up your shit. Get the fuck out of my rental.
> Tommy: Wait. I lost my temper. It's… it's nothing. I'm sorry. See? See? I ain't mad anymore.
> Sam: Did you not hear me?

> Tommy: You're my brother, Sam. You said that you...
> Sam: I'm sick of you. All right? It's over now.
> Tommy: You're the only one I know around here. Where am I supposed to go? (3.11)

He shoots Tommy, but is punished with anger management classes and Tommy's physical therapy bills. Tommy becomes a burden, stumbling pathetically into Sam's bar with a fake limp to mock him daily. The Shadow has become a heavy drain on his life. Neither trusts the other and each envies the other. Tommy is Sam's dirty secret, one he cannot share with his friends.

> Sam: I do crazy things like shoot people! Do you have any idea how much I wish I'd never done that?
> Tommy: Probably not as much as me.
> Sam: Oh, you gotta be kiddin' me. Well, this worked out great for you...All your sins are washed away! Livin' high on the hog at Maxine's house! And I'm just the stupid son of a bitch that shot his own brother! (4.2)

Tommy gets to be the safe, protected child with a loving mother, and Sam is abandoned once more, forced to be the adult without a family. His struggle for support and redemption in the form of his parents and younger brother has failed, as he thinks.

> Sam: I got nobody.
> Tara: You got me.
> Sam: Do I?
> Tara: I'm here, aren't I?
> Sam: Nobody knows me.
> Tara: It's not like you make it easy.
> Sam: Yeah, people think of Sam, as like, "Oh, yeah. Yeah, he's nice." "Yeah, I'll go ask him to do some inconvenient shitty thing and he'll do it, because he's such a good guy." Or, "Yeah, I'll... I'll treat Sam like a cow pie. He won't mind. He's so nice." (3.11)

His one release, as the beginning of season four reveals, is shifting with his own kind, and falling for one of them in particular. He's made peace with his animal side at last. Shifting with his support group means getting positive, healthy acceptance as he celebrates his powers alongside his new friends. His neglected inner child is only getting started, however.

As the Shadow, Sam's neglected rage, fear, and primitive emotions, Tommy strikes out. Tommy acts on Sam's hidden desires as kills their evil parents, a source of stagnation, poverty, and lawless exploitation. The Shadow is also a catalyst for growth. Only out in the woods, helping Tommy bury their parents, does Sam confess that he killed two people himself. The two literally grow closer through this experience, until Tommy is able to turn into Sam.

Tommy in Sam's body lashes out and voices all of Sam's resentments. He fires Sookie for never showing up, and seduces the beautiful but hesitant Luna. While polite Sam "the pushover" is letting Sookie take time off and playing Barbies with Luna's daughter to make himself endearing and nonthreatening, part of him longs for a steamy, selfish seduction, as Tommy accomplishes in Sam's form.

Later, Tommy, the shadow, battles Marcus, the barrier that stops Sam from being with Luna. Just as Tommy falls, critically injured, Sam and Luna make love at last. Tommy's sacrifice has done its job. Sam and Alcide finish his fight and Marcus dies—at last, Sam can have Luna and her daughter.

Luna is a guide to deeper wisdom for Sam—her name suggests her connection with the moon, as does her shifter nature. When she turns into Sam in "Someone that I Used to Know" (5.8), she acts like him, though with greater shifter perception. Working together, he is the angry threatening one, she, the intuitive one. When he makes peace with her and she returns to herself, it's as if the perceptive Sam is absorbed back into everyday Sam. Through knowing her, Sam becomes much wiser and more loving as he adopts Emma as his own.

Literally naked and unarmed in the Authority's dungeons, Sam and Luna use their creativity and magic to save Emma in season five. This is the "deep magic" of Narnia or the natural magic of love and faith pitted against the Authority. Sam negotiates with Bill and spies on the world above while Luna guards Emma in the basement—conscious and subconscious, upper world and lower world, are united with the single goal of protecting the inner child.

"A child made in the underworld is a magic child who has all the potential associated with the underworld, such as acute hearing and innate sensing" (Estés 431). The arrival of the Divine Child represents a new way of perceiving the world and a new level of consciousness. They succeed in escaping with the precious child, but Luna dies as a sacrifice. Now Sam has been guided to a new level of consciousness with a new mission—protect Emma. He may have failed with Tommy, but this far more innocent and sweet child needs him as no one ever has. Friends turn to enemies as the werewolves try to claim her and Sam must take Emma on the run.

Sam also makes a new ally as he's thrown together with Nicole Wright, who's on a mission to persuade shifters and weres to come out. Sam is on the edge of becoming a leader to his larger community, not just his bar but the entire world of shifters. By the very end of season six, he's become the mayor of BonTemps, discovering a risky plan for his community's survival: everyone—vampire and human (one assumes he's mainstreaming as part of the latter) must enter a symbiotic relationship and embrace togetherness against the evil of Hepatitis V. Under Nicole's guidance, he's become an activist.

Though Merlotte's has been renamed, Sam is more in charge than ever, expanding from his bar to becoming protector of the entire town. Brian Buckner explains that Bon Temps is returning to its small town unity in the seventh season, with the end of season six heralding the change:

> It's going to end awesomely. I think you're going to feel that the show is going to return to its roots and it's going to feel like it's about a gang of people in Bon Temps. We're going to try to condense the number of stories we are telling and really make this feel like we're coming home. (Keveney, "HBO's 'True Blood' Going Back")

Alcide

As a season three Sookie struggles to be faithful to Bill, who's broken up with her and committed to his maker, Lorena, Sookie meets Alcide and Debbie. Alcide is presented as Sookie's mirror, someone undergoing exactly what she is. They commiserate together and Alcide escorts her into were society. There, they both experience being outcasts in a world of addicts and gang members.

Alcide is the only male close to Sookie who doesn't try to exploit or seduce her, though they acknowledge romantic feelings and even act on them very briefly in "We'll Meet Again" (5.4). (At the time, he's glamoured into disliking her, suggesting that glamour may wear off or have less effect on weres, as they end season six together.)

He rescues her from the vampires, following all her commands to give her what she desires—Bill safe, until he feeds off her and Alcide helps Tara abandon him in the sun and get Sookie to a hospital. From then on, Alcide remains available to help Sookie with tasks, including locating and corralling a drunken Eric. As such, he's an animus figure or sidekick for Sookie, aiding her when she's incapacitated and providing constant support.

For Alcide, the third and fourth seasons follow his obsession with Debbie, as he struggles to get over her then make their relationship work just as Sookie struggles with Eric and Bill. Once again, their confusion and doubt mirrors each other. Still, he's reflecting Sookie rather than beginning his own arc—all of his story exists in relation to hers. As season four ends, Sookie shoots Debbie, the cheating unfaithful lover who poisons relationships. With that, Sookie is ready for a fresh start.

By season five, Alcide is no longer merely a reflection of Sookie—he's begun his own journey. Alcide spends the season on a quest to find where he belongs—after killing the previous packmaster, who is a force of corruption and greed, he turns himself over to the pack to take responsibility for his actions and save Sam. However, he refuses to rule the pack itself. Upon hearing that they're addicted to V and have a corrupt pack master, Alcide changes his mind and challenges J.D. The werewolf Rikki becomes his lover as well as his second and he begins to be won over to the concept of a good pack with the werewolf community beside him. However, he attempts an honorable fight with no civilian casualties, and he loses.

Depressed, he goes out into the wilderness to return to his roots in the figure of his father, who is the embodiment of werewolf to Alcide. "The only way to beat him is to play by his rules," his father says. Adding that he's always done what's necessary to survive, Alcide's father gives him superior vampire blood—symbolically the magic potion of pack and family instead of servitude. Armed with it, Alcide returns to the pack. In this fight, he uses the dark power of the unconscious—vampire blood—as well as his strength and moral courage. After defeating J.D., he tells them all:

> We're wolves. We respect ourselves. We respect our pack. We respect nature. Without exception. We do not surrender to nihilism. We do not take advantage of those who are younger or weaker than we are....Tonight, we choose Pack. (5.12)

As such, he establishes himself as the new, better leader.

He begins the sixth season enjoying the perks of being packmaster, from young women to savagery. As he devours J.D.s' arm and engages in a threesome, Rikki notes that he's still on the V...an ominous beginning as Alcide gives in to all his dark impulses. Soon enough, his drive to protect the pack leads him to kidnap Emma and battle Sam for her because Emma is a werewolf not a shifter. As he focuses his pack's energy on battling a little girl's adoptive father and an organization that seeks to help shifters and weres, he's becoming the savage he once hated.

Once again his father intercedes, counseling Alcide then watching from the shadows as Alcide spares Sam Merlotte and allows Emma to go to her grandmother. "You were either going to make the worst or best decision of your life, either way I wasn't going to miss it. I am proud of you, son," Alcide's father says. It may be this new level of caring that endears him to Sookie and finally gives them a chance to be together.

Jason

"Jason's so comfortable with his body, it's just part and parcel with who he is," comments his actor, Ryan Kwanten. He adds that Jason "just tends to fly by the seat of his pants" (Wilcott 50). Of the eighteen explicit sex scenes of season one, ten feature Jason. Anna Paquin discusses his role with Michael Martin of *Interview Magazine:*

> MM: It's a sexy show. But what's interesting to me is that the guy playing your brother is the one who's gratuitously topless and naked, kind of like the women in '80s horror movies.
>
> AP: We take his clothes off a lot. As the season goes on, the nudity gets shared around, but in the first couple of episodes, he carries the brunt of that.
>
> MM: What did you and the other women in the cast think of the guy playing the naked-bimbo role? Payback?
>
> AP: It is kind of funny. It is a very sexy show. All of us girls are running around in shorts that barely cover our behinds. Yeah, he's naked a lot, but when you have a body like that…I mean Ryan [Kwanten] has, in all fairness, a ridiculously nice physique, so I don't think he minds too much. (Martin)

Jason's bad relationships are a search for something deeper than meaningless sex, though his search fails. Jason begins the series literally having sex with his latest shallow relationship. (In the books, Sookie's fairy great grandfather Niall mentions Jason's only fairy power is attractiveness to the opposite sex.) He is hyper-masculine, an athlete and construction crew worker with sex appeal. He's "effortlessly charming and not the sharpest knife in the drawer" (Ball). However, he discovers this girlfriend to be the first in a series who have had sex with vampires, whom they found alluring and dangerous. At the same time, his sister takes up with a vampire, his grandmother is overly friendly with that same vampire and finally dies because of his presence. At every turn, Jason feels threatened and outcompeted as the vampires win over Jason's human women.

He finds himself envying the vampires and seeking to compete with them until he overdoses on V. After, he begins consuming V regularly until he meets Amy, who introduces him to his spiritual side. She is his Anima, a feminine influence in his life who builds him up and increases his spirituality as well as his self-confidence. At the same time, she has a destructive, femme fatale side as she goads him to kidnap Eddie and then she makes him an accessory to his murder. Eddie is a mentor of a sort, and Jason, lacking a male role model, eagerly listens to his advice and regrets his death.

Following this, he loses Amy and believes himself guilty of her murder. He gives up the drugs and resolves to be a better person, while still mourning Amy and Eddie. As Eddie notes, "Comes a point in life when you realize everything you now about yourself, it's all conditioning. It's the rare man who truly knows who he is" (1.9). Discovering this is what Jason must do.

Jason's first interest in being a solider appears during Bill's speech about the Civil War. He appears entranced by the idea of being a hero or just finding a greater cause to believe in. However, shellshocked Terry beside him emphasizes that the search for glory has consequences.

In season two, Jason feels lost enough to attend the Church of the Sun, where he confronts his guilt over Eddie's death and voices his hatred for Sookie's choice of boyfriend. It seems like a place of spiritual salvation and cleansing, along with the vanguard of a war against the vampire race. Though Jason begins by insisting a vampire genuinely loves and respects his sister, the manipulative Sarah Newlin persuades him that if their "kind never existed, the people you love would still be alive" (2.3). Though her logic is shaky, she wins him over with emotion, and he soon succumbs to lust for her as well.

At camp, Jason becomes their hero and a natural leader with his competition, aggression, and hatred for the vampires. However, he discovers a world of hypocrisy, bigotry, and lies when he offers honesty as he's been told to do and is met with murderers preaching unrealistic rhetoric. The camp, which insists on honesty, has kidnapped his sister and ignores his protests that he's not involved in her plot.

And what is the American Dream for boys like Jason but success, a hot blonde girlfriend (the married Sarah Newlin will do), and the ability to shoot lots of people while being entirely righteous in doing so? As with most dreams, though, eventually one has to wake up. Thanks to his connection with his more thoroughly grounded sister Sookie, Jason managed to escape the Fellowship before it was too late. (Mamatas 68)

In the midst of this, he finds one true thing he can believe in—his sister. Armed with his paintball gun, he storms the church and rescues her, then flings the preacher's silver ring back into his face. After, Jason admits to Bill he was wrong and hugs him. In a world of confusion and pain, Sookie and her judgment are something he can cling to.

This training from the misguided fundamentalists has shown Jason the path he wants for his future. Back in Bon Temps, he realizes that he (along with Andy and Sam) must save the town from the maenad.

Jason: Then we have got to be the law. Guys, I read a book about this. This is Armageddon. This is the Oral History of the Zombie War. We need weapons, lots of them....Time for thinking is over. It's time for action.
Andy: Maybe Sam's right.
Jason: Has he been to Leadership Conference? Has he had paramilitary training? (2.11)

Afterwards, Jason's mature and heroic, convincing Andy (at least partly) that they are heroes even if no one else knows it. However, he carries his hero image too far when, as he thinks, he saves Andy by shooting a distraught Eggs. Suddenly Andy is the town hero and Jason is accepted as a police officer, with a meaningful job that can provide an outlet for him. Everyone gets what they wanted and nothing is right again.

In season three, Jason confronts his own shadow, one of the self he once was and could have been: Kitch is the new hot quarterback, surrounded by adoring young women and sports scouts. "He's got the best arm of any kid in Bon Temps since...

well, since you," Hoyt reports. Jason finds the boy's arrogance and skill disconcerting, since the teen's exactly a mirror of himself from a decade before. There's another more disturbing parallel between them.

> Jason: You don't need luck, Kitch. You're on V.
> Kitch: I'm not saying I am, but if I was, so what?
> Jason: V's a illegal substance. That makes you a criminal, a drug abuser and a cheater…I'm taking you down, boy. I'm gonna tell your coach, your mom and daddy, and your principal…That ain't fair. I was an athlete out there. I didn't get help from nothing or nobody but my team. That's the way it's supposed to be.
> Kitch: Look at the pros. Everybody's taking something. No dope, no glory.
> Jason: My record stands, asshole. You're no athlete. You never will be.
> Kitch: Well, that's funny. See, there's a scout from LSU coming to the game especially to hand me a scholarship. See, I won't have to stay here and join the chain gang like you. (3.11)

In the days of vampire society, the rules have changed and Jason is the one who never got a break. However, confronting the arrogant teen of V is cathartic, like confronting his past self and recognizing how far he's grown.

A larger problem is his guilt over killing Tara's love and his fear of being found out. Once again, hypocrisy is taking over his life. He and Andy begin a conspiracy to conceal the truth about Eggs' death. In the midst of Jason's misery, he encounters another Anima, or feminine spiritual guide, in the form of Crystal Norris. As with Amy, a girl believes in his total worth and he falls completely in love. However, Crystal is as flawed as Amy. As a were-panther and a girl from Hotshot, she is the savage animal to Jason's civilized self. She teaches him about the forest, where they meet and make love, but she convinces him to betray the DEA and break the law, as Amy once did. Once again Jason is caught between a desire to obey the law and become a morally good person versus his need to break civilized rules and find wildness, love, and freedom.

VALERIE ESTELLE FRANKEL

Amy's kidnapping and murder of Eddie was morally wrong as well as criminal. However, Crystal's desperation to protect her innocent little siblings from the police who will split them and put them in foster care is murkier. Jason is convinced that he will be doing the right thing by betraying his coworkers and breaking the law, so he acts, taking a more complex moral position as he matures.

As season three ends, Jason finds himself saddled with an entire family of children as Crystal leaves him in charge. "I have come to love each and every one of you, and I know you love me, too," he says after a year of caring for them (4.2). The tables have turned between him and Andy—Andy is hooked on V, and Jason has taken his vow to go straight seriously. He's a real police officer, holding the place together as Andy falls apart.

His sister returns from her time in fairyland, but Jason's stable life crumbles when Crystal returns. Jason is knocked out, chained to a bed, and transformed into a were-panther, or at least the family's best try. As all the young women rape him, his hidden fear is brought to life—he is valued only for his body, not for his deeper self. Though he leaves his latest adventure traumatized and absent a girlfriend, as always, he's once again grown wiser. "Every bad thing that's ever happened to me is because of sex," Jason realizes after his experience (4.5).

The panther is a type of black leopard—leopards symbolized early female deities and often accompanied them (Shepherd 179). The ancient Greeks believed their sweet breath lured other animals to their deaths (Shepherd 179). Leopards were actually associated with the maenads because of their great leaping power, and Dionysus wore a panther skin. As such, Crystal and her family represent wild nature, a departure from society's rules and a time of madness, much like Maryann's parties.

When Jason escapes them, he's severely wounded, and Jessica saves him with her blood. His near-death and return sets him on a new path once again: He finds himself so attracted to Jessica that he loses his best friend by pursuing her. Among the many archetypal females he courts, Jessica is the femme fatale, the predatory princess. This is emphasized when she shows up at his door as sexy goth maiden in a red cloak, corset, and little else.

Their relationship is destructive—Hoyt leaves forever and demands to be glamoured into forgetting Jason as well as Jessica. In the sixth season, Jessica's visiting Jason at the same time as Sarah Newlin returns gets her thrown into the concentration camp. For Jason, she will always represent his infidelity toward Hoyt, so he can't bear to be with her. "There were times, hell yeah, definitely love. It just got so screwed up with Hoyt and everything," he tells her (6.5).

At the same time, he acknowledges to Sarah, "Listen, you always seem like a nice lady, aside from the crazy and the hate but I ain't just the same dumb kid you met at the Fellowship" (6.5).

This self-hatred for betraying his best friend may be fueling him at the end of the fifth season as his hatred turns outward, toward Jessica and all vampires. Jason, struck by the Elder's fairy power, finds himself hallucinating his parents. However, both push him toward hate, even as Jessica and Sookie plead for understanding. "Vampires made you orphans. Learn from it," his father tells him (5.12).

Though this is a hallucination, possibly triggered by dark forces, it reflects the conflict within Jason. Life was much simpler when he could honestly hate vampires, rather than having to take their side against the US government. He's being drawn into the grey areas where Sookie lives and protects her supernatural friends. And it's a far more difficult place for straightforward Jason to exist. When Jessica is captured, Jason sets aside his hallucinations and joins the governor's troops, turning from a brainwashed shadow of himself to a man imitating that racist shadow self. He tells his sister:

> Hey Sook, listen, I messed up real bad with Jessica and I gotta go fix it. I just got so bent out of shape the last couple of days, hatin' on vampires but that ain't who I am and that ain't who I want to be so I'm going to make it right. (6.5)

In the camp, however, he undergoes multiple torments. Sarah forces him to watch Jessica's attempted rape, then she turns him over to the female vampires. Violet claims Jason as hers, telling him their bond will last beyond their imprisonment.

After their escape, Jason still feels bound to her, and he has come full-circle, from a man who hated Sookie's bond with Bill to one who shares it with his own vampire lover. She even subjugates him in a one-sided relationship—Jason, who slept with every woman in town is now bound monogamously to a woman who's spent 178 nights making him earn her trust…some might call this true karma.

Lafayette

"You walk into every situation all flash and fire. You expect them to adapt to you," Eric complains. "That's not salesmanship. It's ego" (3.4). Indeed, flash and fire define Lafayette, with the larger-than-life personality that kept him a show regular, though his character died at the end of the first book.

In his first season, Lafayette does what he likes, buying and selling V and trading sexual favors, exploiting and being exploited as he wishes, all without consequences. In many fans' favorite Lafayette moment, he reacts to racist customers complaining that a burger may have AIDS by charging among them and force-feeding the burger to one. He notes, "It ain't possible to live unless you crossin' somebody's line" (1.7). His house and wardrobe are both a perfect mixture of who he wants himself and others to perceive him to be. It appears he lives the exact life he wishes.

However, his many jobs don't bring him wealth, as it's finally revealed all his money from legal and illegal jobs is going to pay for his insane mother's care. Further, all the consequences appear at once when Eric takes his revenge for Lafayette's sales. He kidnaps him and chains him in a basement. There, Lafayette is stripped of his personality—the flamboyant clothes as well as the brash attitude. He bargains for his life, willing to be a vampire and thus Eric's literal slave for all eternity. He does the unspeakable when he digs with his fingers into the body of a man he knew for the metal joint that might free him. In his attempts to escape, he's shot and further tortured before Sookie bargains for his release. She herself has to offer her services whenever Eric wants them, binding herself irrevocably to him in the first of several bargains between them. Though Lafayette escapes, he too isn't free of Eric.

Eric in many ways is a shadow for Lafayette. Both are flamboyantly sexual, willing to display themselves or even trade themselves sexually to get what they want. "I think Eric has locked him in and they'll forever have [a link]. Now he's taken so much of Eric's blood, Eric knows exactly where he is all of the time. He will probably be Eric's little henchman for a long time," Lafayette's actor Nelsan Ellis reveals (Wilkes). However, this plot never fully resolves itself as it fades into the background of the vampire conflict in Mississippi.

In the third season, Lafayette meets Jesus Velasquez, a practicing Brujo. When they take V together, they discover that both their ancestors used magic (3.10). Lafayette sees truths he doesn't want to know about his friends (like the parentage of Arlene's baby) as well as seeing Jesus in a demon mask. In fact, masks and what lies behind them become a major theme of the Jesus-Lafayette arc:

> Ruby to Lafayette: You haven't got your mask...I see you. My son is shining through. And he [Jesus] did this to you? (3.9)

> Jesus: Well, how many other people have you let see behind your mask before?
> Lafayette: Just you. (4.2)

Lafayette's entire personality is performance: overacting, demanding attention. However, with Jesus, he can be himself and channel the deep power he's never explored—the power that comes from the real him.

Jesus takes Lafayette on a magical journey to the brujo of Mexico, Jesus's grandfather. Jesus's grandfather makes him find a sacrifice—in this case, a rattlesnake, and then allows the rattlesnake to bite him. This awakens, not Jesus's powers, but Lafayette's.

However, as Lafayette's possession from a ghostly murder

victim shows, Lafayette's gift is a burden—something that makes him a victim as well as a source of power, much like Sookie's fairy blood. Lafayette uses his gift to see Marnie battling the spirit she's captured, but he's helpless when a spirit tries to possess him. Of course, this is a foreshadowing of a more deadly possession—Marnie takes over Lafayette and murders Jesus. Jesus transfers his power to Lafayette before he dies, and this moment of facing death (his boyfriend's rather than his own) changes Lafayette forever—he will need to master his demon side before it destroys him.

Raelle Tucker, the episode's writer, explains that Jesus appearing and being okay with his death "releases Lafayette from the guilt. Lafayette is now a medium and Jesus is a spirit. I think it'll be interesting to see where that relationship goes."

In the following season, a traumatized Lafayette pours bleach into the food he's cooking. He gazes up at a mirror and sees Jesus's demon mask. At this moment, Lafayette's angry, powerful shadow is lashing out. When someone doesn't explore their personal magic or dark side, when one bottles up all the anger and dark feelings, he is not taking the time to be moody and angry, to connect with the shadow. Thus it can unexpectedly take over the entire personality as it does in this scene.

Lafayette and his mother are both visited by the vision of Jesus' decapitated talking head. Ruby Jean understands that Jesus is "in trouble" and "with an evil man." The talking head functions as an oracle in Celtic and Greek mythologies, among others, as Orpheus and King Bran of Ireland both advise their followers through a bodiless head. As such, Jesus has become an otherworldly wise man, instructing those left behind.

Jesus's grandfather, Don Bartolo, turns on Lafayette, trying to claim the powers for his own child. However, when Bartolo's wife kills him (possibly for trying to interfere with their unborn baby), Lafayette is freed from the weight of the past and allowed to keep the magic. Another mentor is gone, and Lafayette must rely on himself thereafter. In the car, Jesus' spirit appears to him like a vision of consolation and forgiveness. Unfortunately, this relationship too is not strongly resolved, as once again

Lafayette's arc is minimized in favor of others.

Lafayette continues to have magical spikes when he's emotional, and he's helpless against possession, as shown in season six. Both issues indicate that he needs to learn control over his powers. This will be his task in future seasons, as, like Sookie, he must become someone who can use his powers instead of being exploited for them.

Jessica

Jessica the inner child is questing to define herself. She's a vampire, a daughter to Bill, a girlfriend to Hoyt then Jason then James, a rebellious teen and a mature woman. Each comes with changes of costume and attitude. Freud described this aspect of the self as the least conscious, the cluster of basic drives like fear of death, panic, and desire. She's the Id personified—impulse and emotion without control. The Id "knows no judgments of value: no good and evil, no morality" (*New Introductory Lectures,* 107). The Id is also the great reservoir of libido. The whole town of Bon Temps—French for "good times"—seems to stand for the Id (Poole 81).

> Vampire Bill's deadly embrace makes it possible for Jessica, the pious ingénue, to do what comes naturally. She puts the "vamp" in vampire—what a pain in the neck for prospective mother-in-law Maxine! And in a grand mal catharsis, Jessica lets loose long-suppressed human desires: she attacks dear ol' dad—revenge is best served hot! (Hirschbein 132)

Her confusion echoes the human condition, battling her impulses as she tries to make moral choices. "I did an unspeakable thing, and I don't know why god doesn't strike me down right now, unless god is Bill. I don't know, I don't know anything," she notes after killing the fairy girls (6.5).

While Jessica feeds uncontrollably on humans, from the truck driver to the men she cheats with at Fangtasia, she's also the character who falls sweetly in love with Hoyt (though her fangs keep popping out at embarrassing moments) and follows her heart toward him then Jason and James.

As she evolves, she seeks more beyond her everyday life, playing at normal with Hoyt. She finds herself sneaking into Fangtasia, with and without Hoyt, seeking danger and blood beyond her stable relationship. At last, it collapses. Episode writer Brian Buckner explains:

> Jessica's growing up. She was a nice Christian girl...[Now] she's fighting primal urges. She doesn't want to go. She doesn't want to betray her relationship with Hoyt. She just has to. When I brought her into the club, my desire was to have her hunt...She transforms to a more provocative and more aggressive vampire.

After dumping Hoyt, however, Jessica becomes much more powerful.

When Jessica appears to Jason on Halloween, dressed as a seductive red-cloaked corseted maiden, Jason embraces the passion she's offering, but he's stunned when she reveals she doesn't want a serious boyfriend. "She's changing and she wants to experience things," Raelle Tucker, the episode's writer, comments, and points out how unusual it is for the man to want the relationship and the woman to just want sex. Jessica's Halloween costume is a statement about who she wants to become, a girl comfortably with her sexuality, breaking out of her role as Hoyt's good-girl girlfriend to seduce Jason the stud.

Season five begins with Jessica getting the keys to the vampire castle. Bill leaves to deal with the Authority, and Jessica finds herself flaunting Bill's wealth and power. When Reverend Newlin comes for Jason, Jessica calls herself an older vampire and "pretty much the queen" with her royal father out of town. She's no longer just an ingénue—she's the new queen of vampire-land.

When Newlin threatens Jason, she becomes the first female vampire on the show to insist, "He is mine" about anyone. Indeed, the support staff at Bill's "palace" rush to get her more beer. In red and purple, she parties like a teenager for the first time. At last she's doing what she wants and acting like a vampire in control rather than one being pushed around by her urges. She has her own friends and a chance at college as the other young people tell her. "People go to college to become big and powerful, right? Well I already am," Jessica smiles (5.1). She makes out with a teenage boy and tries to hide her jealousy as Jason goes off with a college girl. She also manipulates Bill to try saving Jason, rather than the tearful tantrums of the past. Though she's ageless, she's growing up.

In the concentration camp, James sacrifices himself rather than hurt her. His declaration that she's not a monster, just at the moment she feels most worthless, touches her. She asks him:

> You know when they brought me in here I had just done just about the worst thing I have ever done as a human or a vampire and I thought that if I was a monster then we all must be but then you did something so selfless. Why didn't you do it, it would've been so much easier for you if you would have just did it? (6.7)

She struggles to save him as well as herself and embraces him as the gentle, loving animus to her own monstrous side. James in turn tells her she makes him want to live forever. Convinced he can guide her to a higher spirituality, she says, "It's not fear, everything about you is good and decent. You have this humanity coursing through you and in my last days that's what I want you know. That's what I want to leave the world feeling a part of" (6.7). With James by her side, she survives meeting the sun and finds freedom. Their relationship is an embodiment of light and goodness, vampirism as life-affirming rather than only death.

By season end, she's accepted her terrible act and finds a way to make amends for it. She knocks on Andy's door, fully prepared to be shot if that's what he wishes. She tells him, "I want to give you your girls back. But I can't. The only thing I can give you now is some kind of peace of mind" (6.10). With her vow of protection, she acknowledges there's no way to pay the debt and makes a moral choice instead of an impulsive one.

Tara

Tara, like Sookie, undergoes several heroine's journeys. In season one, Tara deals with the bad mother. "Out all night doing all kinds of God-know-what! You the devil, child! You ain't no child of mine!" she cries when she's drunk (1.3). Lettie Mae is like everything bad out of Tara's childhood, but for Tara there's a worse fear:

> Tara: You think I can end up like her.
> Lafayette: There's some darkness in this family, Tara. My mama, your mama. But they ain't strong enough to beat it. We are. (3.2)

Midway through the first season, Miss Jeanette performs an exorcism and instantly transforms Tara's brutal mother into her opposite, the good mother. This split of mothers is an issue out of depth psychology:

> A baby considers the mother part of the self—the baby cries, and the mother is instantly there to feed it, as if they're one self. But if the mother yells, punishes, is slow to offer comfort, the baby cannot comprehend that its mother, source of all love and goodness, also has a less-than-perfect side. So the small child polarizes, sees her as the Good Mother with kisses, and the bad one with spankings. This "Terrible Mother," as Jung calls her, is the wicked witch of fairy tales.
> But to the child, these are more than two aspects of the mother—they're two aspects of the self. This is called the Jungian Mother Complex, and it is one of the earliest and most central forces in a woman's psyche. The Good Mother is perfect kindness, love, and protection. As such, she has few defenses. (Frankel, *Buffy* 155-156)

Tara longs to love the good mother, but deep within, she knows the bad mother will return. Worse yet, she fears the dark mother within herself, which she sees whenever she gazes at Lettie Mae. She undergoes her own exorcism, a small descent as she struggles to release her own darkness. A child appears in her vision and she stabs the child, trying to banish her misery, pain and fear. The girl's eyes are black, foreshadowing the black-eyed minions of Maryann that Tara soon will join. She's small and vulnerable, like Tara's most inner self. "She's just this little flower, this wounded child that needs to be taken care of. And that's where the mouth is coming from, and all that quickfire language," comments Tara's actress, Rutina Wesley (Buchanan).

However, even after Lettie Mae is healed, she abandons Tara in a jail cell. At this moment, the good mother appears once more, this time as a new character: Maryann bails Tara from jail and whisks her off to a perfect life at her mansion. Wesley adds:

> Everything that Tara's always wanted to do, or the clothes she's wanted to wear, or even the makeup she wants to be a lady, that's what Maryann is allowing her to have. She's taking care of her in a way that her mother hasn't. (Buchanan)

Maryann tells Tara, "If you took care of yourself for once, instead of protecting her, she'd still be your mother, and you'd just be happier (2.1).

Miss Jeanette of course is the false seer, who only claims to connect with the great beyond. The Maenad Maryann, by contrast, can actually do so. She kills Miss Jeanette and takes her place. Maryann is a best friend, protector and benefactor—everything to Tara. Maryann supplies her with a home and pretty clothes, but also Eggs, the perfect boyfriend. Maryann also defends Tara to her mother:

> Maryann: Miss Thornton. Maryann Forrester. I've heard all about you. What a rare opportunity this is. I've always wondered what it would be like to gaze into the eyes of someone so devoid of human compassion, that you would abandon your own child when she needed you most.
> Lettie Mae: What?
> Maryann: Just as I thought. Emptiness. Nothing inside. It's always something out there that gets all the blame or the credit. Whether it's Jesus or Jeanette.
> Lettie Mae: Who are you?
> Maryann: What I can't believe is that your daughter still manages to feel any love for you. Since you've abused, betrayed and forsaken her love since the moment she could

feel. That's extraordinary. She's a hell of a girl. Come on. Let's get you home. (2.1)

Maryann, Tara's powerful shadow, speaks in Tara's voice, saying all the things Tara's too weak to say herself. She tells off the towel guy who interrupts Tara's perfect kiss, encourages Tara to fall for Eggs, does everything, in short, Tara's buried self wishes. Rutina Wesley, notes:

> We're watching Tara go through growing pains, so to speak. We're seeing her gain her own sense of womanhood—she never was able to become a woman, I feel, because she had to take care of her mother. Now, though, with her mother out of the picture, Tara can kind of be herself and find out who Tara is and fall in love. (Buchanan)

"I got sucked in, cause she made me feel like I was part of like a family or something," Tara says (2.12). Sookie responds by reminding her she still has family.

However, Maryann is feeding off Tara, drawing her into the savage cult. Sookie, the best friend who represents faith, trust, and conscience, pulls Tara out of her possessed state and banishes the maenad with her friends. The mad, savage, benevolent mother is gone.

This however leaves Tara with Lettie Mae. She finds the worst possible solution for Tara when Eggs is killed: She calls the preacher to lecture Tara that it all happened for a good reason, she ignores her daughter to flirt with him, and she's self-absorbed enough that she doesn't realize Tara is attempting suicide. "Get out of the way. With a mother like you, it's a miracle she ain't tried this years ago...You failed this girl for the last time, you hear me?" Lafayette roars (3.2).

Tara's Animus Growth

Tara deals with her mother in the first season, but her romantic adventure basically arcs through the second season. For Tara, Eggs is the immature Animus, offering her passion without any grounding—when he discovers that he killed people for

Maryann, he has a complete emotional breakdown and waves a knife at Andy Bellefleur. Jason kills Eggs, and his death sends Tara into a destructive and even suicidal spiral. The lesson has been learned that emotion is not enough.

Jason is the one to kill Tara's good but unstable boyfriend Eggs, then her wicked boyfriend Franklin. The first time, he destroys Tara's world, driving her to attempt suicide. The second time, he saves her. "You saved my life last night. You've been saving me since I was a little girl," Tara notes (3.10). In the same conversation, Jason reveals that he killed Eggs, and Tara's hero-worship for Jason dies. The part of her that relied on a man to protect her vanishes, and she realizes she must save herself in the future.

Tara's cousin Lafayette is a force of initiative and planning. He's the one to save Tara from Maryann and then again at the beginning of season three when she attempts suicide. However, he mostly offers actions—he physically makes her throw up the pills and then drives her to see his mother. His power is deeds, not words. Even his speeches convincing her not to hurt herself again concern what he'll *do*.

> Tara: I didn't plan it. I just saw the bottles, and I thought, "Enough." I deserve some peace.
> Lafayette: And I deserve to plan your fucking funeral? Spend the rest of my goddamn life blaming myself? ... Life ain't not having problems, Tara. It's about being able to deal with the ones you got.
> Tara: Well, obviously, I can't.
> Lafayette: You can and you will, if I gotta drag your narrow ass through this world kicking and screaming. Look, the Buddhists weren't lying when they said life is suffering. It don't mean you get to check out early and leave me here.
> Tara: What are you doing?
> Lafayette: First I'm gonna get some food in you. Second, there's something you need to see.
> ...
> Lafayette: Hooker, if you ever try to pull the shit you pulled last night again, I swear, your ass is gonna get a room next to Ruby Jean. And I'm gonna make sure the motherfucker spooning your peas ain't half as hot as Jesus. Is you feeling me?

Tara: Yeah, I'm feeling you. (3.2)

Franklin is more thoughtful and considering, reflecting his vampire nature. As Godric notes in the same episode where they meet, "A vampire is never at the mercy of his emotions. He dominates them" (3.2). Though he's a tyrant and a monster, he teaches Tara to be cunning and manipulative, to trick her way out of his bed and captivity.

After Franklin, Tara leaves town and changes her identity: She's now Toni, a professional fighter with a lesbian girlfriend. However, her attempt to run away from everything in Bon Temps fails. "I thought if I could make you believe in it, maybe I could too," Tara says to Naomi. (4.6)

Tara dies saving Sookie at the end of season four, and then she rises from her grave, pink shirt smeared with red blood. The young vampire is a savage, like the normal Tara with all civilization stripped away. This is shadow-Tara, everything she's feared, hated, and longed for in herself.

> "When Alan [Ball, the series creator] first told me, I just freaked out," the actress recalls, laughing. "While we were setting up to do another take, he just pulled me into a corner and said, 'Hey, we're really excited about something, and I hope you will be, too. Tara's going to be turned.' And I was like, 'What? That doesn't mean that I'm dying, does it?' Because normally when a character gets turned, they've got one more death and then that's it; they're gone." (Crook)

However, Tara's life as a vampire brings her a powerful new beginning.

Tara and Pam

"Would you toss a newborn baby in a gutter?" Eric asks (5.3). Based on Pam's treatment of new vampire Tara, that's exactly what Pam would do given the chance. As such, she's the ultimate destructive mother straight out of the fairytales. She's spent the series threatening and attempting to kill Tara, along with her friends Sookie and Lafayette.

> Just as the "good mother" is the life giver, the wicked stepmother or "Terrible Mother" takes life from the most innocent, her own children whom she should cherish. Yet this viciousness can sometimes be a response to patriarchy, in a world in which women are most valued for youth, beauty and fertility. (Frankel, *Girl to Goddess* 269)

Pam, of course, is consumed by jealousy as Eric continually chooses Sookie over her. However, when she sees a despairing Tara attempt suicide, Pam commits to her utterly. "Becoming a maker is an eternal commitment. Throwing that away is sacrilege," Eric told her long ago (5.3). Even as she has complex feelings toward her own maker, who's rejected her, she embraces his teachings and a complex relationship begins. Tara's actress relates:

> "I asked, 'Ooh, do I get to dress like her? Do I get to be sexy?' Kristin is just awesome, and as long as I got to dress like Pam, I was OK with it," Wesley says. "As an actor, something like this is the meat, the thing that keeps you inspired and challenged to do something new. I decided that, as a vampire, Tara would walk in a slightly different way, kind of like a panther, and her voice was going to be lower. There was a whole physical transformation that I tried to work in, but it's still Tara. (Crook)

Tara starts working in Fangtasia, and there her buried rage is allowed an outlet—she is a vampire now.

"I think Pam and Tara are very similar. Whether that makes for a happy relationship or not I'm not so sure...but sure makes for a fun one to watch on TV," comments Kristin Bauer van Straten (Pam) (Halterman). When Tara curses out a racist customer (in this case, her high school peer), Pam tells her off as her other employers have, but later, Tara finds the woman chained in the basement, begging to be Tara's slave. Pam encourages her dark side as no one else has. For the first time, someone understands Tara's rage and affirms it, tells her that she has a right to be angry.

"A lot of time Tara feels misunderstood but she's like no,

this hurts, when you're being treated like that and talked to like that, so I think it's nice that Tara finally gets some satisfaction," her actress comments ("Vamp Vindication" 5.8). Tara responds to Pam's harnessing her dark strength, and kills the new sheriff to protect their home. In turn, Pam takes the blame for Tara's crime, much to Tara's surprise. Tara has a genuine protector in her mother/sister/lover at last.

When Pam leaves Bon Temps to find Eric at season end, she tells Tara to watch over Willa—Tara thus changes from daughter to mother. Willa introduces herself six months later as Tara's "friend"—it's unclear if their relationship has become sexual. Meanwhile, at long last, Tara and Lettie Mae make peace. As Lettie Mae cries, "Let me nourish my child!" she offers her daughter the safety and comfort self-reliant Tara has gone without all her life. Becoming a vampire and then a member of the new vampire-human community has allowed Tara to cycle back to the beginning and find her childhood good mother once more.

BLOODSUCKERS ON THE BAYOU

Mythology

Vampires of the World

Across the world, blood represented the life force. As such, it had power, whether one took it or offered it freely. In ancient times, some tribes would drink an enemy's blood to gain his power. Worshippers smeared statues of their gods with animal blood, and the concept existed that one had to give in order to receive—the word "sacrifice" comes from Latin *Sacrum facere*, "to make holy." Likewise, the word "blessing" comes from the Old English *bletsain,* to sanctify through sprinkling of blood (Walker 170). In the Bible, blood represents life itself. Dracula in the Bram Stoker novel quotes Deut. 12:23: "The blood is the life."

Blood is seen when Jesus and Lafayette use a girl's murder to fuel their magic and Jesus paints himself with her blood and even tastes it. The horned god Maryann summons is also a blood god. Lafayette explains, "Only through the blood will he come" (2.12).

Vampires as the vengeful, blood-drinking dead appear around the world as well, as vampires seek to take life power from the living. Vampires have physical bodies, unlike ghosts—some believe they are like demons, who take over a host's body and possess it, while others believe they are the original body returned to life. John Heinrich Zopfius in his *Dissertatio de Uampiris Seruiensibus,* in 1733, says:

> Vampires issue forth from their graves in the night, attack people sleeping quietly in their beds, suck out all their blood from their bodies and destroy them. They beset men,

women and children alike, sparing neither age nor sex. Those who are under the fatal malignity of their influence complain of suffocation and a total deficiency of spirits, after which they soon expire. Some who, when at the point of death, have been asked if they can tell what is causing their decease, reply that such and such persons, lately dead, have arisen from the tomb to torment and torture them. (qtd. in Summers 1-2)

The word "vampire" originates from the Turkish and Polish *upior,* witch, the Mediterranean vam-pir, blood-monster or the Russian *wampira,* associated with blood-drunkenness. Almost every culture has a myth about the angry dead, risen from the grave to suck the blood of the living. The Sumerian *ekimmu* was a restless spirit that returns in the night. *Xiang shih* were Chinese corpse hoppers who flew, seduced women, and transformed into wolves. The vrykolaka "wolfskin" can't enter a house uninvited but has a glamour of compelling charm. It leaps on people and smothers them with its crushing weight.

Other Vampires

Abchanchu Bolivia
Adze West Africa
Al Armenia
Ala Turkey
Algul Arabia
Alp Germany
Ataru Ashantiland
Asasabonsam Ghana
Aswang Manananggal
   Philippines
Bajang Malaysia
Baobham-Sith
   Scotland
Baital-Pachisi India
Bhuta India
Brahmaparusha India
Bruxsa Portugal
Callicantzaro Greece

Cihuateteo Aztec
Chindi Navaho
Churel India
Dachnavar Armenia
Danag Philippines
Doppelsauger
   Germany
Draugr Viking
Ekimmu Babylonia
Empusa Greece
Eretik Russia
Gayal India
Glestigs Celtic
Kathakano Crete
Krasyy Thai/Laotian
Lamia Babylonian
Langsuior Malaysia
Leanan Sidhe Celtic

Loogaroo Granada
Mara Denmark
Mrart Australia
Mullo Gypsy
Nachzehrer Germany
Nagasjatingarong
  Indonesia
Nakaq Peru and
  Bolivia
Nelaspsi Slovakia
Nukekubi Japan
Obayifo Ghana
Obji Kashubs
Ohyn Poland
Otgiruru-Herero
  SW Africa
Owenga Guinea
Quaxates Mexico
Palis Persia
Penanggalan Malaysia
Pijawica Croatia
Pisaca India
Polong Malaysia
Pontianak Indonesia
Pret India
Revenant Europe
Sarkomenos Crete
Sigbin, Philippines
Soucouyant Trinidad
Strigoiaca Romania
Strigori Romania
Sukuyan Trinidad
Talamaur Polynesia
Tanggal Indonesia
Tengu Japan
Tenatz Bosnia
Tin-tin Ecuador
Tlahuelpuchi Mexico

Uahti Amazon
Vetala India
Vieszcy Kashub
Vrykolakas Greece
Wume Togo
Xiang shih China
Yara-Ma-Yha-Who
  Australia
Yuki-onna Japan
Yuruga Persia

Battling Vampires

Beheading is popular, though vampires are extraordinarily strong and fast: catching one while sleeping or trapped indoors during daylight hours gives the slayer a definite advantage. Fire cleanses and destroys the corpse so thoroughly that nothing remains to reanimate. Bonfires, originally called Bone fires, were lit to purify tainted livestock and cremate the bones of a vampire. The usual concept involves destroying the body utterly, so a spirit cannot return to it.

Vampires leave their graves at night to feed on the blood of the living. When dug up, their corpses appear fresh, even flushed with life, from the lifeforce they've absorbed from others. Some believe only the prone vampire in his grave can be killed, a superstition likely deriving from the vampire's incredible strength while awake. Even headstones were originally created to prevent the dead from sitting up!

Mirrors are said to reflect souls, hence the superstition that vampires do not reflect in a mirror derives from their lack of soul to be reflected. From the link between mirrors and souls comes the concept of bad luck from breaking a mirror and the tradition of covering mirrors after a death, so the soul will not be trapped on earth. Water reflects, thus there is a tradition that crossing water will trap the vampire's spirit. The eyes too can reflect and trap a person's soul, a concept that is brought to life in the vampire's mesmerizing gaze. The tradition of closing a dead person's eyes exists through today, originally inspired by this concept.

Mourning was often seen as a necessity to prevent the angry ghost from returning. The living would dress differently and cut their hair short, a tradition originally intended to disguise them from the dead. If a corpse was unburied or even left unattended, it might rise again.

As all other demoniacal monsters the Vampire fears and shrinks from holy things. Holy Water burns him as some biting acid; he flies from the sign of the Cross, from the Crucifix, from Relics, and above all from the Host, the Body of God. All these, and other hallowed objects render him powerless. He is conquered by the fragrance of incense.

Certain trees and herbs are hateful to him, the whitethorn
(or buckthorn) as we have seen, and particularly garlic.
(Summers 131)

Garlic is used as a blood purifier and is used for protection
through Europe and Asia. The pointed stake, traditionally of
hawthorn or rosewood, is actually a tool of exorcism. Originally
it was used to pin the vampire down and prevent it from rising
during the ritual. In Romania, wild rose petals and wolfsbane are
popular for dispelling vampires, along with the more famous
garlic.

Vampire hunters made a living traveling medieval Europe
and battling the undead. "These pros may range from clerics, for
whom fighting all manner of evil is an expected part of the job,
to people whose destiny aims them at the undead; to half-
vampire offspring with a real case of paternal resentment"
(Maberry 50). They used the tools above to rid the world of the
walking dead and restore it to the mortals.

Literary Vampires

Charlaine Harris says she "followed the classical Dracula
pattern, with a dash of Anne Rice's and Laurel K. Hamilton's
[mythologies]" ("Charlaine Harris Answers Questions from her
Fans" 308). Harris cites Lovecraft, Edgar Allen Poe, Jane
Austen, and Shirley Jackson as influences on her cross-genre
work (Wilcott 26). She also colors her books with in jokes—It's
mentioned that Anne Rice really interviewed the vampire Louis,
just as Stoker really met Dracula "at a weak moment" ("Dracula
Night" 44).

In history, Vlad Dracul was born in 1431 in Transylvania.
His father was made a knight of the Order of the Dragon,
complete with a black cape for ceremonial wear. His native
people called him "Dracul," Dragon, after the insignia on his
shield, but some called mistook it for the image of the devil, as
the dragon represents the forces of darkness in Christian
iconography. Dracula, senior, was proclaimed prince of
Wallachia, but on his father's death, his half-brother seized the
throne. He finally led an army against the nearby Turks and
seized his throne at last. Young Dracula adapted to court life,

but after the family patron died, young Dracula was taken prisoner by the Turks. He remained there for some years, able to see their techniques of medieval torture up close.

At age twenty-five, Dracula escaped, raised an army, and regained his throne. Many stories exist of his brutality toward his own peasant class—of torture, mass execution, and above all, impaling. Deaths were said to reach between 40,000 and 100,000—a fifth of the population of Wallachia. While the stories are incredibly grisly, they were for the most part written and spread by Dracula's enemies in a negative press campaign, leaving their truthfulness possible but unsubstantiated. After his death, his coffin was never found, and rumors spread that he had been seen, unaged, for centuries afterwards. From all this sprang the legend Bram Stoker seized for his novel.

Vampire stories existed before *Dracula,* but it was the one to truly fire the public's imagination. In the gothic genre's early popularity, John Polidori's *The Vampyre* (1819), written at the same party as Mary Shelley's *Frankenstein,* casts its charismatic Lord Ruthven as rich and seductive, but unrepentantly evil. *Varney the Vampire* (1847) likewise delighted British readers. *Carmilla* (1872) by Joseph Sheridan Le Fanu features Dr Hesselius's quest to save the innocent Laura from her mysterious friend Carmilla, a girl drawn to her romantically as well as savagely. Carmilla's obsessive pleas ("You are mine, you shall be mine, and you and I are one for ever") are echoed in the vampires Sookie meets, along with Pam's lesbianism and the naming of the Hotel Carmilla. In 1897, Bram Stoker published *Dracula* during a gothic revival, and the cool, aristocratic Eastern European vampire was born.

A series of films followed, especially the famed Bela Lugosi one: "After 1931, whenever millions of theatergoers would think of the Count, they would see Lugosi's face" (Bibeau 106). Afterwards, Christopher Lee played Dracula in a long series of films, but they made less of an impression on vampire history. It was not until the emergence of horror comics in the 1940s that the vampire appeared in adolescent fiction, and even then the move was met with resistance (Waltje 87). The controversy saw the vampire banned from teens for another two decades.

1967's *Dark Shadows* introduced the first sympathetic television vampire. He was meant to be short-lived, but was popular enough that the studio kept him on. As bookseller Daniel Seitler notes, "Dark Shadows came out of the '60s gothic romance revival—it was not strictly about horror. This special combination has been rediscovered recently and helps contribute to the success of two modern vampire franchises— *True Blood* and especially the *Twilight* saga" (qtd. in Maberry 80).

> Contemporary radical feminist vampire writers have found in the figure of the vampire marvelous potential for radical re-appropriation. In their work the status of vampires as cultural indices and metaphors has been re-valued, aligning them with a new feminist carnivalesque. They infuse the age-old figure with new life. Writers such as Anne Rice, Poppy Z. Brite, Jewelle Gomez, Katherine Forrest, Angela Carter and Sherry Gottlieb have all re-appropriated the figure of the vampire and use it to question life and death, gender roles and romantic myths. Engaging with the challenge that conventional horror offers, of female victims and sexually voracious monsters, they have revived and reinterpreted the vampire to their own radical ends. (Wisker)

Harris too has Sookie questioning her role in the world as she dates paranormal vampires and weres, resenting their high-handed treatment. Anne Rice and Chelsea Quinn Yarbro were the first authors to create "sexy vampire protagonists" Lestat and St. Germain, which eventually led to the ones popular today. Now vampires are smooth and fascinating as a matter of course, paranormally glamorous. "The vampire today is now Frank Langella, the handsome and sensitive (far more sensitive than his human counterparts) vampire in John Badham's *Dracula,* the pensive Miriam in *The Hunger,* the inquisitive Lestat and St. Germain, or the saucy and sexy Vampirella" (Senf 10).

Anne Rice wrote about an angst-filled vampire in New Orleans and his search for family. She sees the vampire as "a handsome, alluring, seductive person who captivates us then drains the life out of us so he or she can live. We long to be one of them, and the idea of being sacrificed to them becomes rather romantic" (qtd in Steiger, *Real Vampires* 12).

The *Anita Blake: Vampire Hunter* series by Laurell K. Hamilton is a hard-boiled detective series with a female action hero complete with supernatural gifts. Anita's vampires and werewolves exist alongside the ordinary folk and are gaining rights. When one commits crimes, however, she's there with her necromancy power to battle them. Romance slowly builds as well, as Anita grows closer to the occult world.

In many ways, Sookie's vampire romances can be compared to the arcs of female slayers, as they struggle to determine morality in an uncertain world. Buffy the Vampire Slayer is a teenager and Anita Blake, 24. Like Sookie, both are pretty, petite, physically skilled, and smart. They're known for witty, sarcastic dialogue. Also like Sookie, they are born with powers that make them vampires' natural enemies and are more mature than their peers, especially from all the death they've seen. Neither slayer feels she has room in her life for romance. Because of their slaying, both spend a great deal of time with nonhumans. "Neither woman intentionally seeks a lover among her enemies, but for each a variety of factors culminates in an unexpected and powerful attraction to the predators she is sworn to destroy" (Leon). For young women who keep so much of their lives secret, their unnatural boyfriends are important, because the girls can share their entire lives with them. Both characters start with strict black and white morality that degrades into confusion as they encounter more of the supernatural. Sookie, too, changes from a very moral young woman to one who's busily hiding bodies and remaining silent while her supernatural friends murder and feed off the guilty.

Further, Sookie becomes a slayer herself as she changes from a polite doormat of a waitress to a woman who will defend her loved ones with stakes and rifles. After being tortured by fairies and emerging stronger in the books, Sookie realizes she'd indeed be willing to kill another human being. She immediately longs to, as she puts it, "run to the nearest gun store to make a purchase, don some black leather, and high heeled boots, and reinvent myself as a kick-ass heroine" ("Small Town Wedding" 41). By the twelfth book, she calmly invites an enemy inside, thinking to herself that "there were lots of weapons in the kitchen" (*Deadlocked* 216). She removes all the sweet potatoes from a boiling pot, and then hurls the water at her adversary. No one will ever mess with Sookie in her own house again.

Buffy is thought to be the precursor for many popular vampire series. Dreamed up by its producer Joss Whedon as a blonde frivolous teen with a destiny and incredible slaying powers, it redefined teen television and led to many WB coming-of-age shows like *The Vampire Diaries*. As Andy Burns of *Biff Ban Pop!* notes, "Joss Whedon managed to make the things that go bump in the night palatable to viewers that may never have watched a horror film before. Without *Buffy the Vampire Slayer*, there would be no *Supernatural* or *True Blood*" (qtd. in Maberry 71). It also explored vampire day-to-day life, as did its spinoff, *Angel*. Vampires were Other, but also beloved main characters living in town, forcing the humans to adapt.

Likewise, "mystery or suspense is an important element in a large number of vampire books" (Guiley, *Vampire Companion* 65). Often, as with Sherri Gottlieb's *Love Bite* or Richard Laymon's *The Stake*, a body or bodies turn up, and occult detectives must locate the vampire responsible. Female detectives like Nancy Drew go back to an older tradition, and Sookie fits easily among them:

> Late nineteenth- and twentieth-century girls' novels, and the annuals/comics of the nineteen-fifties and sixties are full of stories which feature young girls with energy and power who use the tactics normally found in male sleuths to track down crime, right wrongs, and return order...But the schoolgirl novels, comics and annuals developed a very different kind of version of young womanhood, energetic, adventurous plucky, imaginative—boy-like in fact. Sexuality was not an issue here, and the adventurous young women fought singly or together to re-establish a moral status quo. (Wisker)

Most of the Sookie Stackhouse novels contain one or more murders early on, with a secret villain like René that Sookie must uncover.

As vampire and detective fiction evolved, *Forever Knight* came to the television, with a vampire detective solving crimes to balance the scales of his past misdeeds. Many other shows came after, all with the reluctant, angst-filled vampire:

Forever Knight 1992-1996
Kindred: The Embraced 1996
Buffy the Vampire Slayer 1997-2003
Angel 1999-2004
Moonlight 2007-2008
Blood Ties 2007-2008
Being Human UK 2008-present
Being Human US 2011-present
The Vampire Diaries 2009-present

Twilight is famous for sweeping a decade of teens into paranormal romance novels, including the Sookie Stackhouse books. These stories show becoming a vampire as positive and also show the angst-filled vampire determined to have a hands-off relationship, a comforting romance for many younger readers. Stephen King explains:

> In the case of Stephanie Meyer, it's very clear that she's writing to a whole generation of girls and opening up a safe kind of joining of love and sex in these books. It's exciting and it's thrilling and it's not particularly threatening because they're not overtly sexual. A lot of the physical side of it is conveyed in things like the vampire will touch her forearm or run a hand over skin, and she just flushes all hot and cold. And for girls, that's a shorthand for all the feelings that they're not ready to deal with yet." ("Exclusive: Stephen King")

Many cite *Twilight* as making teen readers feel safe in post-9/11 culture—Edward is protective and determined not to seduce the heroine—it is she who must take charge.

Indeed, vampires represent the forbidden, the crossing of taboos. They drink blood, prowl at night, seduce young women, do all the things condemned as "evil." They are often burned by the presence of holy symbols or the nurturing sun. Yet the heroine, bored with ordinary men and ordinary troubles, finds herself drawn into his seductive world.

Vampires have always been a way for the culture to explore what frightens or disturbs them, from the gothic shadow of straight-laced Victorian society to the fears of terrorism and safety today. Deborah Ann Woll (Jessica) notes that on the show, "We talk a lot about the nature of being a freak and being different....it can create villains and it can create heroes."

True Blood tackles racism and sexism in the old South, along with the vampires as metaphor for homosexuality. It's been called the most inclusive series on cable television, with six LGBT characters.

> The first episode aired in September of 2008, just months before the passage of California's Proposition 8. That November, as Californians voted to alter the state constitution and deny marriage rights to gay citizens, millions of viewers were watching the plight of "vampire Americans" in Bon Temps, Louisiana. The show's opening sequence featured footage of Civil Rights marches in the South juxtaposed with a roadside sign that declared, "God hates fangs." *The New York Post* quickly labeled the show a "gay-rights analogy" and writer Alan Ball was voted one of *Out* magazine's "Power List" of influential gay Americans. (Laycock)

As noted previously, this angle has been explored in the nineteenth century *Carmilla* and before. The main character of the 1984 *I, Vampire* by Jody Scott begins, "To remain young and adorable, I must drink six ounces of human arterial blood once a month. This is not an ethical choice. I was born this way. If society wants to kill me or cure me, that's not up to me" (qtd. in Senf 1). The emphasis on birth not choice echoes homosexuals' pleas for acceptance and equal rights in a society that's only gradually becoming tolerant.

While the vampire today is sexy and desirable, his barely-controlled savagery and bloodthirstiness remind fans that he will always be Other—it remains for society to decide whether to flee or embrace this hidden shadow of ourselves.

Shifters and Weres

> There are apparently two kinds of the two-natured: shifters, who can change into any type of animal, and weres, who

change into only one type of animal. By far the most numerous clan is the werewolves, and they're so proud of that that they just refer to themselves as Weres, with a capital W. (Harris, *The Sookie Stackhouse Companion* 221)

Sookie succinctly sums up were life in her world. But this concept wasn't made up for her novels. Around the world, were-animal myths can be found. Fox spirits are scattered through Asia, from Chinese *huli jing* to Japanese *kitsune*. The Netsilik Eskimos had protective familiars or *tunraq*, much like Sam's pet collie. Were-hyenas are known among the Persians, Ethiopians, Sudanese, Moroccans, Berber people, and the African Bornu Empire. The Bangwa people of Southwest Cameroon each have their particular animal. Among the Shan tribe of Thailand, if a person has the power of *phi phu*, he can change into were-animal form. The Egyptians prayed to animal-human hybrids, like jackal-headed Anubis and "for Christians in the Middle Ages, images of Anubis reinforced folk legends of were-jackals that attacked unwary desert travelers" (Steiger, *The Werewolf Book* 9). The Azande of Africa stayed on guard against the *andandara*, malevolent wild cats that mated with human women. The Berserker warriors of Northern Europe believed they actually transformed into bears in the midst of their battle rage. Native Americans had many legends of people intermarrying with or turning into animals, from the Inuit dogmen, the *adlet*, to the animals found on spirit quests.

The indigenous people of Chiapas State in Southern Mexico have *naguals*, animal guides that live in a parallel world beside them. Father Juan Bautista, traveling through Mexico in 1600 writes:

> There are magicians who call themselves teciuhtlazque, and also by the term nanahualtin, who...transform themselves to all appearances, into a tiger, a dog or a weasel. Others again will take the form of an owl, a cock, or a weasel; and when one is preparing to seize them, they will appear now as a cock, now as an owl, and again as a weasel. (Brinton)

In most myths, shapeshifters had to surrender completely to the animal of choice, but they also had to have enough sense of self to return.

Were-cats were common in Africa and Asia. In Mesoamerica, the powerful animal of choice was the were-jaguar or were-panther. An elite class of Aztec warriors were called "jaguar knights," complete with animal skins, and were-jaguars appear frequently in their art. The Aztecs and Mayans taught that were-jaguars could be rid of cultural restrictions and inhibitions by straddling the two worlds.

In medieval Europe, the wolf was the animal of choice. Wolves are associated with bravery and fierceness as well as with devouring the darker forces of evil (Shepherd 182). They are scouts and also guardians of the underworld. As such, they represent barriers or guides to characters who cross over. They're creatures of the forest, strong predators. Werewolves according to Sookie are "the roughest elements of the two-natured community," likely to do construction work or ride motorcycles (*Dead as a Doornail* 58). The legend of the *loup-garou,* man-wolf, comes from New Orleans tradition and the tale of a collective of butchers and their families slaughtered by a mysterious beast (Steiger, *The Werewolf Book* 18).

The show tries to put its were-animals in historical context. As Eric notes:

> There is a pattern. The Turks told folk tales of shape-shifting jackals at the fall of Constantinople. The Aztecs were decimated by disease from the conquistadors' war dogs. Each time, there's been wolves, fueled by vampire blood. I nearly found him [Russell Edgington] in Augsburg in 1945. His wolves were in the service of the Wehrmacht. He disappeared after the war, and I—I thought he finally met the true death. Now he's returned. (3.9)

In fact, Hitler was fascinated by werewolves and named a secret commando group for them (Steiger, *The Werewolf Book* 134, 218). In *True Blood, Wolf Hunter* by J.L. Benét, and a few other fictional adaptations, those werewolves end up being literal.

Luna, Sam's lover, confides in the shifter group to reveal she has her own conflicted past—she shapeshifted into her mother once.

My father's side is Navajo. Like, old-school Navajo. My bedtime stories were not written by Doctor Seuss. I had to fall asleep listening to "The Legend of the Skinwalkers." ...According to the Navajo, Skinwalkers were horrible, evil witches, whose powers allowed them to transform into any animal on earth...including other people. But they were said to be able to gain their powers in one way only. They had to kill another shifter. Another member of their own family...It was crazy. And scary, at first. But then I was like, "I get to be my mom." I mean, I never got to meet her, and then, yeah, I was her. (4.2)

Jeffery Pritchett of the *Examiner* interviewed J.C. Johnson of *Crypto Four Corners* on Skinwalker beliefs. He explained:

The Skin Walker, for whom he is, and what he does, transforms him/her self into an emulation or imitation of an animal. Some wear hides, some transform, some travel in spirit form. Every intention I've witnessed, is that they bring evil and misery, and do not benefit the Diné Navajo and continue to keep them prisoners of darkness and superstition.

To Become One of them:
1. Sacrifice a loved one, or sibling, child— someone close to you.
2. Bring in the body to the group, that they may practice some necrophilia, and then feast on some of the body parts. Later they will take some of the organs, and make powders and potions.
3. You now begin your apprenticeship with a practicing leader.
4. Your family and children are no longer yours. They become part or eventually die.

Skinwalkers can be differentiated from humans by the vertical movement of their ears and tails (Guiley, *Encyclopedia* 313-314). Their initiation process, of killing a family member, is of course considered evil. These Skinwalkers or Witches are believed to injure others out of anger, spite and revenge, qualities that appear on the show, particularly in Tommy.

Fairies

Bill: Fairy is but one of the names.
Sookie: What other names are there?
Bill: Finodrerr. Ellyllon. The Old People. Aliens. (3.10)

From the earliest ages the world has believed in the existence of a race midway between the angel and man, gifted with power to exercise a strange mysterious influence over human destiny. The Persians called this mystic race Peris; the Egyptians and the Greeks named them demons, not as evil, but as mysterious allies of man, invisible though ever present; capable of kind acts but implacable if offended.

The Irish called them the Sidhe, or spirit-race, or the Feadh-Ree, a modification of the word Peri. Their country is the Tir-na-oge, the land of perpetual youth, where they live a life of joy and beauty, never knowing disease or death, which is not to come on them till the judgment day, when they are fated to pass into annihilation, to perish utterly and be seen no more...All over Ireland the fairies have the reputation of being very beautiful, with long yellow hair sweeping the ground, and lithe light forms. They love milk and honey, and sip the nectar from the cups of the flowers, which is their fairy wine. Underneath the lakes, and deep down in the heart of the hills, they have their fairy palaces of pearl and gold, where they live in splendour and luxury, with music and song and dancing and laughter and all joyous things as befits the gods of the earth. (Wilde)

Fairyland, the dazzling yet perilous "other world" is permanently ingrained in Western thought (fairyland in the eastern tradition is quite similar, but *True Blood* seems to come from the traditional Irish fairyland.) All Sookie experiences, from the lake entrance, to the beauty, to the foul goblins and hazardous fruit, are traditional signs of fairyland. One collector of tales notes:

Fairies live in a subterranean parallel universe of their own that is often entered via holes in the ground, a mountainside, or a hill, and also in subaqueous castles entered via a lake or river. Fairyland is not one of everyday experience; it is Other, and only visible from time to time to special adults and children, not because the viewers will it, but because they somehow fall upon it by chance (Mack XXIII)

The prohibition against eating fairy food is the most famous rule—fairyland is derived from the Other Realm—symbolically, the underworld—and eating from the realm of the dead means one has willingly abandoned the world of life and must remain apart forever. Sookie's Grandpa Earl, who ate of the fruit and returns home only to crumble to dust, is a motif seen in fairy legends across the world.

> If you enter, beware of eating the fairy food or drinking the fairy wine. The Sidhe will, indeed, wile and draw many a young man into the fairy dance, for the fairy women are beautiful, so beautiful that a man's eyes grow dazzled who looks on them, with their long hair floating like the ripe golden corn and their robes of silver gossamer; they have perfect forms, and their dancing is beyond all expression graceful; but if a man is tempted to kiss a Sighoge, or young fairy spirit, in the dance, he is lost for ever—the madness of love will fall on him, and he will never again be able to return to earth or to leave the enchanted fairy palace. He is dead to his kindred and race for ever more. (Wilde)

Time delay or time speeding up is another common trope, emphasizing the difference between the mortal and immortal worlds. Amnesia is common as well.

> Sometimes one may thus go to Faerie for an hour or two; or one may remain there for seven, fourteen, or twenty-one years. The mind of a person coming out of Fairyland is usually a blank as to what has been seen and done there. (Evans-Wentz 38-39)

Fairies are one among many creatures of fairyland. As Claudine notes, fairies "...are your basic supernatural being. From us come elves and brownies and angels and demons. Water sprites, green men, all the natural spirits...all some form of fairy" (*Dead to the World*).

Fairies are portrayed in the books as beautiful, with pointed ears and glossy skin. While most can pass for human, humans are instantly attracted to them and vampires can barely resist the urge to drain them to death. Watching vampires react to Claudine, Sookie thinks that "it was like watching cats that'd suddenly spotted something skittering along the baseboards" (*Dead to the World* 22). In the books, they're vulnerable to lemon juice as well as the traditional iron.

> Sometimes a man hearing the merry music and seeing the wonderful light within would be tempted to go in and join them, but woe to him if he omitted to leave a piece of iron at the door of the bower on entering, for the cunning fairies would close the door and the man would find no egress. There he would dance for years—but to him the years were as one day—while his wife and family mourned him as dead. (Evans-Wentz 88)

On the show, fairyland and its beautiful fairies are revealed as an illusion over a goblin-filled, barren land. Mab has been gathering the halfbloods for her own whims, and Sookie's attempt to escape soon turns deadly.

Queen Mab

In fairyland, Sookie meets "Queen Mab." She's mentioned in Shakespeare's *Romeo and Juliet* as "The fairies' midwife, and she comes/In shape no bigger than an agate-stone" (I:iv:54-55). Since her Shakespearean debut, she's appeared as queen of the fairies (like Shakespeare's other queen, Titania) in many fantasies.

However, Mab is not Shakespeare's invention. The Warrior Queen Medb of Connaught appears in the Ulster Cycles. She was a powerful queen who demanded that any prospective husband be without fear, meanness, or jealousy...because she intended to take lovers. Eventually, she appointed her bodyguard and lover Ailill king as soon as he'd killed his predecessor. When she coveted a bull that would ensure she had equal goods to her husband, she dragged them all into an epic war.

While the heroine here was a mighty queen, many consider her an ancient earth goddess whom the king had to marry to establish his reign, before her identity morphed into this tale. In ages past, "A king could only ascend to the throne by symbolically uniting himself with this goddess through the exchange of a libation. As the goddess handed the cup to her husband, she also gave him her permission to rule over the land" (Condis 39). In Irish Gaelic, the name "Medb" means "she who intoxicates," like the related word "mead" (Condis 39).

> In fact, her story had already been tampered with…It was altered and adapted by the Christian monks in medieval Ireland who sought to preserve it. Their redactions transformed Medb from a sovereignty goddess into a power-hungry, sexually promiscuous, and illegitimate mortal queen; however, even the redacted version of Medb found within the pages of the monks' manuscripts is haunted by hints of the goddess Medb, moments in which her former power shines through. (Condis 32)

Many neo-pagans today worship her as fairy queen or ancient Celtic goddess of libations and rulership.

> Of the great female figures of Ireland, Maeve was probably the most splendid. Originally a Goddess of the land's sovereignty and of its mystic center at Tara, she was demoted in myth, as the centuries went on and Irish culture changed under Christian influence, to a mere mortal queen. (Monaghan 204)

Wiccans

Witches were persecuted heavily in Europe in the fifteenth century and after. Most were women, a great number were leaders, independents, widows, and property owners. After their torture by the male witchfinders, their property went to the church or to the witchfinders themselves. Confessions under duress, hearsay, and rumor were accepted as evidence, and the world spiraled into cruelty and injustice. The primary handbook, *Malleus Maleficarum*, written around that time, insisted birthmarks and moles could be proof of witchcraft, and added that women were intrinsically evil. Looking away during questioning, shedding only a few tears, not owning a cross, or not arguing when accused were all taken as proof (Marshall 63).

Neopaganism, also called Wiccanism, is a product of the twentieth century. Margaret Murray wrote *The European Witch Cult* (1926) and *The God of the Witches* (1960), both of which expressed her belief that the confessions during the witch trials were largely true and suggested an organized but secret witch religion. Around the same time, Gerald Gardner wrote guidebooks teaching rituals based in Eastern mysticism, Kabbalah, and British legend, which quickly caught on. By the late 1960's, there were several organized branches of Neopaganism, using folklore, ancient myth, Eastern religion and symbolism to construct an earth religion. Many wiccans believe in magic, which they see as the harnessing and redirection of natural energy to create change in the world. Those who cast spells call themselves witches—not all Wiccans would identify as such. Neither wiccanism nor this witchcraft is Satanic, though its followers may worship a Goddess in place of a god, or balance the genders between multiple deities (Marshall 146-149).

> Basic Beliefs of Wicca:
> The core tenets of most Wiccan systems (and there are many) include the following:
> - Nature, filled with divine power, should be honored and respected. Holidays usually correspond to the seasons.
> - Ancestors should be respected, and there is a path to commune with the spirit world and the ancestors who watch over us all.
> - The Divine is male as well as female, in all of us, not just the priesthood or saints.
> - Do not harm others.
> - Respect the beliefs of others.
> - Everyone is responsible for their own actions and must accept all consequences, good or bad. (Wigington)

Holly carries a "Wiccan first aid kit," as she puts it, salt, sage, and a lock of her aunt's hair (4.12). Salt and burning sage are used to cleanse in the fourth season, by both Lettie Mae and Holly. Herbs and a sacred circle are common tools in Wiccan practice. In European tradition, sage was a cure-all, and its name comes from the Latin *salvere,* to save (Shepherd 250). Salt, as required for human life and a product of the mortal world like bread and iron, was used to drive off demons, vampires, fairies, and all types of occult creatures. It was considered a substitute for blood in ritual, because they taste alike and were both identified with the Mother Goddess's primal sea (Walker 170). As the world's oldest preservative, it was a symbol of purification and rebirth.

Holly is a benevolent figure, seen praying for aid but not generally casting or breaking spells. "Usually I just light a candle and ask the spirits to make sure my boys don't end up in jail or knock somebody up. So far that's worked out okay," she explains (4.12). She is much more a traditional wiccan than power-mad Marnie, and many wiccans interviewed reflect that opinion.

"I'm absolutely disappointed with the portrayal of Marnie," said one self-described witch—a biology professor. "When Marnie gives up her 'power within,' which is a witch's ability to practice the craft without harming others, it allows possession by Antonia who becomes the controlling entity. Marnie lets it happen. It's unconscionable a witch would act this way" (Carr).

"Ethical witches communicate with the dead, not bring them back to life. Crossing these lines was very grave and not something any of us would advocate. She went overboard," RavenHawk, another practicing witch, adds (Carr).

The final circle Holly casts, beseeching the aid of good spirits on Halloween and having them convince Marnie it's time to go on, is more in the spirit of Wiccanism than the aggressive spellcasting and possession of the earlier episodes. Samhain, the holiday that later became Halloween, is the "Feast of the Dead," a sacred day on which Wiccans and Pagans honor the ancestors. It was the end of harvest, when the Celtic year ended and the world went cold and dark. Animals were slaughtered, bonfires were lit, and there may be a tradition of human sacrifice. (Bill and Eric come to loathe the last two of these.) It's a good time to contact the spirit world for advice, protection and guidance because the veil between this world and the next is at its thinnest.

Holly, Tara, and Sookie, three young goddesses of the series, form a circle and beseech everyone who loves them to come protect them. And in a moment that goes straight to Sookie's heart, Adele appears along with the others. As their ancestors save them and gently convince Marnie to travel on, they bless the living women of the series with peace.

The Brujo Tradition

> A fabulous now deceased promoter, "Brujo Mayor" [First Warlock] Gonzalo Aguirre, organized a witchcraft convention in Catemaco, Mexico, in 1970, offering a black mass, row boat races, anthropological discourses and the presence of brujos, witch doctors, shamans, and like ilk. Since then, Catemaco has soared in international and Mexican renown as an asylum for mysticism and witchcraft. The convention is repeated yearly beginning on the first Thursday in the month of March. ("Catemaco Brujos")

Thus it's no surprise Jesus's grandfather is a *brujo*, as he is. The Tuxtlas mountainous terrain was geographically isolated through the 1950's. It's a place of tropical jungles and rare medicines. Once, there were 40 different kinds of Aztec healers and magical practitioners living in the region. Through today, *curanderos* (healers) are trusted with many local problems, and many people entrusted themselves to the *brujos* (witches) as well. An influx of African slaves (with their own jungle background) and the Catholic tradition (which metamorphosized Aztec culture into saint worship) all have their influence, as Cuban *santeria*, Haitian *voodoo*, and Catemaco *brujeria* are closely related. Catemaco *brujos* sell spells nowadays, and they are joined in their profession by *culebreros* (snake bite healers), *chamanes* (local "white" witches), *yerberos* (herbal healers), *hueseros* (a form of chiropractor), *yorbateros* (massage healers), and *parteras* (midwives). For the casual visitor, dozens of herbalists and amulet sellers congregate in the central Catemaco market, though finding more serious practitioners is more difficult.

A Brujo always has his *Nagual,* or a "guardian spirit," such as a coyote or lizard. The earliest description goes back to a Spanish historian as he traveled through present-day Honduras in 1530:

> The Devil was accustomed to deceive these natives by
> appearing to them in the form of a lion, tiger, coyote, lizard,
> snake, bird, or other animal. To these appearances they
> apply the name Naguales, which is as much as to say,
> guardians or companions; and when such an animal dies,
> so does the Indian to whom it was assigned. The way such
> an alliance was formed was thus: The Indian repaired to
> some very retired spot and there appealed to the streams,
> rocks and trees around him, and weeping, implored for
> himself the favors they had conferred on his ancestors. He
> then sacrificed a dog or a fowl, and drew blood from his
> tongue, or his ears, or other parts of his body, and turned to
> sleep. Either in his dreams or half awake, he would see
> some one of those animals or birds above mentioned, who
> would say to him, "On such a day go hunting and the first
> animal or bird you see will be my form, and I shall remain
> your companion and Nagual for all time." Thus their
> friendship became so close that when one died so did the
> other; and without such a Nagual the natives believe no one
> can become rich or powerful. (Brinton)

Much of this matches Jesus's experience, as he was forced to sacrifice a goat as a child, then is told to go out and meet his totem animal as an adult.

The animal that approaches Jesus is the rattlesnake, which bites him and provides a conduit to awaken Lafayette's powers. The rattlesnake is an animal only indigenous to the western hemisphere. Many tribes associated its swiftness with lightning, and thus with the rain and fertility of the earth. The rattlesnake's association with poison and death connects it with transformation: its bite could carry people across the barrier into death and hopefully bring them back. For Jesus and Lafayette, it does just that. Vampires on the show have rattlesnake-style teeth (Ball). As such, Jesus and Lafayette are meeting their inner vampire, their dark side.

Lafayette also notices his boyfriend's jaguar tattoo. "All major Mesoamerican civilizations prominently featured a jaguar god, and for many, such as the Olmec, the jaguar was an important part of shamanism" (Miller and Taube). For some, the jaguar represents the power to face one's fears, or to confront one's enemies. Thanks to the jaguar's size and power, the Aztec, Olmec, and Maya civilizations featured jaguars and were-jaguars in art, religion, and ritual. The jaguar was said to be the hidden sun, the realm of spirituality, twilight and death. In Mayan mythology, the jaguar was the ruler of the Underworld. It was known for perception, especially in darkness. Jesus of course is a figure of perception and magic, then finally death.

The Maenad

> Sam: Maryann is not God.
> Daphne: Well, she's as close to God as we'll ever get. People call her all kinds of things. Kali, Lilith, Isis, Gaia. But what she really is, is a maenad...According to the Greeks, maenads were handmaidens of Dionysus. But they're really a lot more than that. (2.7)

Kali and Lilith, along with aspects of Isis and Gaia, were dark underworld goddesses. They all represented the shadow side of the religion, buried creativity and power along with rage and savagery. Facing the dark goddess involves stripping away life's illusions and confronting the ancient needs and desires beneath. Silvia Brinton Perera comments in *Descent to the Goddess*, "There is a quality of primal rage about her. She is full of fury, greed, the fear of loss, and even of self spite" (35).

The Maenad character began with its classical origins—as her actress Michelle Forbes related, "We talked about Bacchus and Dionysus; what a maenad is, how they're led by appetite, how they thrive off other peoples' appetites, chaos and destruction. But, you know, that was the diving board, but it wasn't the pool..." (O'Connor).

In Greek and Roman myth, Maenads (also called Bacchae) were the worshippers of Dionysus or Bacchus, the god of wine. In Tara's mind when she becomes a devotee, she repeats many names of Dionysus: Bromios, noisy or boisterous; Dendrities, he of the trees; Eleutherios, the liberator; Enorches, the fertility god.

Dionysus was in some ways the most common of the

gods—he was half human in fact, and "an earth-deity, a god of the peasantry" (Willoughby). He had various animal forms including that of a goat or kid.

> By far the most generally accepted and most significant of the animal embodiments of the god, however, was that of a bull. There were a multitude of cult appellatives emphasizing this conception of Dionysus. He was variously addressed as the "horned child," the "horned deity," the "bull-horned," and the "bull-browed." The Argives [Greeks] worshiped him as "the son of a cow" or "bull-born," and the ancient Elean chant addressed him directly as a bull. "Come, hero Dionysus, come with the Graces to thy house by the shores of the sea; hasten with thy bull-foot." So ran the hymn itself, while the chorus repeated "goodly bull, goodly bull." One readily recalls, also, that the residence of the king-archon at Athens, where the sacred marriage between Dionysus and the basilinna was celebrated, was called the boukolion, or "ox stall." (Willoughby 73)

Bulls were associated with moon goddesses like Syrian Astarte and Egyptian Nun. They were an embodiment of nature and source of great physical power. In the ancient Roman ceremony to Mithras, initiates were covered with a bull's blood for its magic (Shepherd 151).

The Bacchae, followers of Bacchus, celebrated their rites with a famous kind of abandon and lawlessness. They would dance to strange music, shouting and waving torches in a great frenzy. In fact, the name Bacchus itself is an epithet or description meaning the noisy or riotous god. Plato remarked that "an immortality of drunkenness seemed to be considered the Dionysian reward of virtue." As Daphne tells Sam on the show:

> Dionysus, Satan. It's really just a kind of energy. Wild energy, like...lust, anger, excess, violence. Basically, all the fun stuff. Maryann brings it out in people. She channels it, controls it. She's immortal, Sam. She never wasn't here, so there ain't no point in fightin' her. You see, you'll never win. (2.7)

> For the Bacchanals themselves, however, the experience
> was something more and higher than drunkenness. It was
> spiritual ecstasy, not mere physical intoxication. The wine
> they drank was for them potent with divine power—it was
> the god himself, and the very quintessence of divine life
> was resident in the juice of the grape. This the devotees of
> Bacchus knew as a matter of personal experience when,
> after drinking the wine, they felt a strange new life within
> themselves. That was the life and power of their god. Their
> enthusiasm was quite literally a matter of having the god
> within themselves, of being full of and completely
> possessed by the god. So they themselves described it in
> their own language (entheos, enthusiasm). They might be
> intoxicated; but they felt themselves possessed by the god.
> The drinking of wine in the service of Dionysus was for
> them a religious sacrament. (Willoughby 75)

In their frenzied worship, the Bacchae would dance and sing in the wilderness and devour the "feast of raw flesh," tearing a goat or other animal to pieces and devouring it. In Crete, to quote Firmicus Maternus, "the Cretans rend a living bull with their teeth, and they simulate madness of soul as they shriek through the secret places of the forest with discordant clamors" (qtd. in Willoughby 77).

In the famous play, *The Bacchae* by Euripides, King Pentheus decides he's above participating in the rites, but he spies on them from the bushes. His own mother, a full participant, tears him to pieces and carries him home in her madness, believing he's a lion. Maryann's mad, delusional worshippers parallel this famous tale. Pentheus's story hints at an older, gorier rite—human sacrifice and cannibalism, as "In its primitive [form] this rite probably involved the sacrifice of a human victim" (Willoughby 77).

> Bacchic experience also caused a break with the customs
> and conventions of ordinary life and a return to the freedom
> of nature. The devotees of Dionysus deserted their homes
> temporarily, wandered free on the mountains, and indulged
> in certain wild, primitive, half-animal passions. Euripides
> gave a picture of the matrons of Thebes leaving their
> homes, their work, their babies even, to wander and revel in

the mountains. They dressed themselves in fawnskins and wound snakes around their bodies.
> Some cradling fawns or wolf cubs in their arms
> Gave to the wild things of their own white milk
> Young mothers they, who had left their babies.

With this return to the life of nature there was mingled a recrudescence of certain very primitive impulses. There was a lust for hot blood and a certain ferocious cruelty in the tearing to pieces of hapless victims. (Willoughby 81)

In *The Bacchae*, worshippers could accomplish great miracles in their sacred madness. The herdsman of Pentheus tells of particular wonders accomplished by the maenads:

> And one would raise
> Her wand and smite the rock, and straight a jet
> Of quick bright water came. Another set
> Her thyrsus [sacred staff] in the bosomed earth, and there
> Was red wine that the god sent up to her,
> A darkling fountain. And if any lips
> Sought whiter draughts, with dipping finger-tips
> They pressed the sod, and gushing from the ground
> Came springs of milk. (43)

Related to Maenads were the Maniai, goddesses of madness and frenzied chaos from which we get the word *maniac*. When Ajax, a great warrior, was denied the armor of Achilles, "the nightmare-fiend of Mania," an ancient moon goddess, took him over, and he slaughtered his own allies and finally killed himself.

The witches' sabat was described similarly to the rituals of Dionysus: male horse-hoofed Sileni, goat-hoofed satyrs, and female human maenads would gather in the wilderness and tear apart those who spied upon their rituals. Thus this was another female sphere, one devoted to shattering rules and conventions, at least for a finite time.

Modern scholars are divided on the source of the practice, with many seeing it as an explosion of the oppression the women lived under, finally releasing itself in orgies and savagery. Others believe it was a female form of spirituality, as the women channeled and became the Great Goddess (Monaghan 203). The desire for oblivion as tied to the release was tied to the ritual, to the point that it's Maryann's strange goal. "She has to believe that she's successfully summoned forth Dionysus… in hope that he will ravish her, quite literally devour her, until she's lost into oblivion," Sophie-Anne explains (2.11).

The Ifrit

In Arabian lore, the ifrit is a vampiric spirit of a murdered man, seeking revenge on his murderer. It rises up like smoke from the victim's blood (Guiley, *Vampire Companion* 23). The word comes from *afara* "to rub with dust." Ifrit are a type of evil Djinn or Genie: Djinn are sentient beings with free will. Some are good, while the *shayātīn*, or demons, are evil and serve Iblis, the devil.

The Qur'an mentions that the jinn are made of a smokeless and "scorching fire" (15:27), but also physical in nature, able to interact physically with people and objects and likewise be acted upon. An Ifrit is mentioned in the Qur'an, Sura An-Naml (27:39-40):

> An ifrit (strong one) from the jinn said: "I will bring it to you before you rise from your place. And verily, I am indeed strong, and trustworthy for such work." One with whom was knowledge of the Scripture said: "I will bring it to you within the twinkling of an eye!" Then when Solomon saw it placed before him, he said: "This is by the Grace of my Lord–to test me whether I am grateful or ungrateful! And whoever is grateful, truly, his gratitude is for (the good of) his ownself; and whoever is ungrateful, (he is ungrateful only for the loss of his ownself).

In early folklore, the ifrit is said to be powerful and difficult to control. Various amulets and the name of God are said to be helpful in banishing it.

On the show, the ifrit haunts Terry as an echo of his guilt for the things he did during the war. As guilt for the deaths consume him, the emotion takes physical form and tries to literally kill him. Magic brings the metaphor and emotion to life, as so often happens in fantasy, especially in Bon Temps.

Lilith and the Vampire Bible

> According to the Vampire Bible, Lilith was created by God in His own image: a vampire. Adam and Eve were created to sustain her, beginning the natural order of humans existing to service vampires. Lilith eventually met the sun at the hands of man, after which her progeny gathered her remains in an earthen jar. (5.7)

The *True Blood* version of the creation story shows Lilith as the first vampire and Adam and Eve as her food source. In Jewish folklore, Lilith is often seen as a demonness or early vampire as she kills babies to sustain her own existence. She was Adam's first wife before Eve:

> After God created Adam, who was alone, He said, "It is not good for man to be alone" (Genesis 2:18). He then created a woman for Adam, from the earth, as He had created Adam himself, and called her Lilith. Adam and Lilith immediately began to fight. She said, "I will not lie below," and he said, "I will not lie beneath you, but only on top. For you are fit only to be in the bottom position, while I am to be the superior one." Lilith responded, "We are equal to each other inasmuch as we were both created from the earth." But they would not listen to one another. When Lilith saw this, she pronounced the Ineffable Name and flew away into the air. Adam stood in prayer before his Creator: "Sovereign of the universe!" he said, "the woman you gave me has run away." At once, the Holy One, blessed be He, sent these three angels to bring her back.
>
> Said the Holy One to Adam, "If she agrees to come back, fine. If not, she must permit one hundred of her children to die every day." The angels left God and pursued Lilith, whom they overtook in the midst of the sea, in the mighty waters wherein the Egyptians were destined to drown. They told her God's word, but she did not wish to return. The angels said, "We shall drown you in the sea."
>
> "Leave me!" she said. "I was created only to cause sickness to infants. If the infant is male, I have dominion over him for eight days after his birth, and if female, for twenty days."
>
> When the angels heard Lilith's words, they insisted she go back. But she swore to them by the name of the living and eternal God: "Whenever I see you or your names or

your forms in an amulet, I will have no power over that infant." She also agreed to have one hundred of her children die every day. Accordingly, every day one hundred demons perish, and for the same reason, we write the angels names on the amulets of young children. When Lilith sees their names, she remembers her oath, and the child recovers. (Stern and Mirsky 183-184)

Thus she became a succubus and demon, preying on the helpless at night. In the wilderness where she dwelt, she had orgies with elemental demons and sand spirits, producing hordes of demon children. "The daughters of Lilith, Adam's first wife, took revenge for his rejection of her by seducing his descendants and drinking their blood. So the sexiness of vampires is nothing new," notes Wilcott (17). She's been tied with vampires in many stories.

Her backstory is first mentioned in *The Alphabet of Ben Sirah*, a book of Jewish mysticism dating back to the first millennium. She derives from older sources: Mesopotamian mythology mentions a Liltu bird perched in the goddess Inanna's garden, and the Lilim, various she-demons. On the show she's accompanied by several bloody Lilim or female demons (called sirens in the script) as she imbues Bill with great power and leads him towards his destiny.

Lilith appears in the ancient mythology of Samaria, Babylonia, Canaan, Persia, and Arabia.

The ancient name "Lilith" derives from a Sumerian word for female demons or wind spirits—the *lilītu* and the related *ardat lilī*. The *lilītu* dwells in desert lands and open country spaces and is especially dangerous to pregnant women and infants. Her breasts are filled with poison, not milk. The *ardat lilī* is a sexually frustrated and infertile female who behaves aggressively toward young men. (Gaines)

She's also found alluded to in the Bible (her name is translated into a screech owl in the King James version of Isaiah 34:11-15).

According to this powerful apocalyptic poem, Edom will become a chaotic, desert land where the soil is infertile and wild animals roam: "Wildcats shall meet hyenas, / Goat-demons shall greet each other; / There too the lilith shall repose / And find herself a resting place" (Isaiah 34:14). The Lilith demon was apparently so well known to Isaiah's audience that no explanation of her identity was necessary. (Gaines)

She's said to live in the ruined desert of Edom and consort with wild animals such as pelicans, vipers, wildcats, hyenas, and satyrs (Marshall 22).

Anti-Lilith mythology is found in the religions of Islam, Judaism and Christianity along with older near-east sects. As such, many see her as the patriarchy's attempt to demonize the strong feminine and turn a goddess into a demon. Today she's considered a feminist icon, based on her determination to be equal with Adam. Many Neopagans say prayers to her and name their daughters for her. A women's magazine and a national literacy program are named for her, and an annual music festival that donates its profits to battered women's shelters is called the Lilith Fair. She is considered one of the dark underworld goddesses of the ancient world, like Kali or Hecate. She is the anti-Eve, no longer man's helpmeet but the source of feminine rage and power, determined to tear down the world in her search for equality and revenge against the male authority.

She spent her time as a life-destroyer, subverting the holy act of intercourse and its design in creating children. Lilith was endlessly fertile, endlessly wrathful at her own children's death. Thus, as she birthed children who quickly died, she maintained the balance of the world. Outside the normal bonds of creation, she became the defiant one, the destroyer ... Without equality, she would destroy earth's infants, its healthy relationships, in payment for her own perished children. (Frankel, *Girl to Goddess* 274)

Lilith encourages the vampire hierarchy, repeating that "Only one can lead us. I choose you" to each of the council, until they begin killing each other. However, she subverts it, as she influences her chosen Bill but doesn't take form and replace him on the Council. She is happy to rule through influence and manipulation, like Salome, the other seductress-murderess, but more successfully.

VALERIE ESTELLE FRANKEL

In Anne Rice's third book, *The Queen of the Damned,* Lestat visits Enkil and Akasha, the Adam and Eve of all vampires. Askasha destroys her mate and abducts Lestat to persuade him to help her create a new world of women, subservient to her, their goddess. Lestat eventually reveals that he is her weak link and that she's deluded, so he turns on her. The Lilith and Bill plot of season five seems to imitate this arc, though Bill succeeds in Lilith's mission for him.

Bill's good lover Sookie, champion of life and beautiful fairy, is her natural enemy. Though Sookie and Lilith never meet, and she has few encounters with "Billith," Bill saves the vampires of his world, descending into the camp and offering them his blood and protection in the sun chamber. He then saves Sookie from Warlow, embodying the triumph of the ancient goddess over the predator as well as the force of death.

Lilith is not shown to have the sanguinista agenda, but she amasses a cult of followers who believe that is her mission. "There are fundamentalists who do believe...that humans are farmed as food, nothing more. Emotional alliances between vampire and humans are blasphemy," Bill's interrogator in the Authority warns (5.2). In other words they are the literal enemies of Sookie's love for both vampires. Fundamentalists among the vampires are against them, just as the Church of the Sun is. It's no wonder Reverend Newlin returns.

BLOODSUCKERS ON THE BAYOU

Conclusion

Though Charlaine Harris recently concluded the Sookie Stackhouse series with book thirteen, *Dead Ever After,* she will be releasing *After Dead* on Halloween 2013. "It's not a novel, but an alphabetical listing of all the characters in the series, or at least most of them—I couldn't get everybody in—with what happens to them after the series is over," she told *SciFiNow.* (Tyley, "Charlaine Harris")

> So there will be Sookie, Sam, Eric, Tara and JB [Tara's book husband] and just about everybody else will be in there with just a little line or two to say this is what happened to them afterwards because I don't want to keep getting those questions for five years after when I have a bad habit of forgetting what I make up at one point so I make up a whole different answer! (Tyley, "Charlaine Harris")

After Dead will also kill off a few of the characters, in a massive epilogue like that of *Lord of the Rings.*

> "The entries are quite brief and some of them include characters that have now died and how they died," Harris continues. "If Alan [Ball] got inspired by my books, I got inspired by Alan's ending for Six Feet Under, where he shows all the characters when they die. But this isn't all about death, they've had a happy life and death is the end of that, inevitably." (Tyley, "Charlaine Harris")

After *After Dead,* Charlaine Harris will create a new series of mystery novels, beginning with *Midnight Crossroad,* set at the titular crossroads in Texas. It will have multiple points-of-view, something different for those who loved Sookie's first-person perspective. As Harris adds, "There's *only one* vampire and he's pretty unusual...He's gonna be a new character; I'm not ever gonna retread any of *those* vampires" (Tyley, "Charlaine Harris"). It's slated for a May 2014 release.

There's also a series of graphic novels from IDW Publishing with new stories—all are supervised by show creator Alan Ball and focus on the *True Blood* characters rather than the book ones. For those eager for more episodes while waiting, they're a good choice.

As for the show, it's been renewed for season seven, and Sookie has yet to pick the one great love of her life. Relationships like James and Jessica's or Tara and Pam's haven't yet had time to flourish, and additional episodes will give the characters time to discover if they can make the matches work. Alcide has a new relationship to manage, as he pulls back from the aggressive road he's been traveling, and Sam will need to choose whether to come out as a shifter even as he guides the people of Bon Temps toward a real "togetherness." The books also offer a fairy war, more supernatural relatives for Sookie, marriages, babies, and many more murders. With thirteen of them, there's plenty of plot for many more years of *True Blood.*

Episode List

Episode Number	Episode Name	Director	Writer
Season One			
1	"Strange Love"	Alan Ball	Alan Ball
2	"The First Taste"	Scott Winant	Alan Ball
3	"Mine"	John Dahl	Alan Ball
4	"Escape from Dragon House"	Michael Lehmann	Brian Buckner
5	"Sparks Fly Out"	Daniel Minahan	Alexander Woo
6	"Cold Ground"	Nick Gomez	Raelle Tucker
7	"Burning House of Love"	Marcos Siega	Chris Offutt
8	"The Fourth Man in the Fire"	Michael Lehmann	Alexander Woo
9	"Plaisir d'Amour"	Anthony M. Hemingway	Brian Buckner
10	"I Don't Wanna Know"	Scott Winant	Chris Offutt
11	"To Love Is to Bury"	Nancy Oliver	Nancy Oliver
12	"You'll Be the Death of Me"	Alan Ball	Raelle Tucker

Season Two

1	"Nothing But the Blood"	Daniel Minahan	Alexander Woo
2	"Keep This Party Going"	Michael Lehmann	Brian Buckner
3	"Scratches"	Scott Winant	Raelle Tucker
4	"Shake and Fingerpop"	Michael Lehmann	Alan Ball
5	"Never Let Me Go"	John Dahl	Nancy Oliver
6	"Hard-Hearted Hannah"	Michael Lehmann	Brian Buckner
7	"Release Me"	Michael Ruscio	Raelle Tucker
8	"Timebomb"	John Dahl	Alexander Woo
9	"I Will Rise Up"	Scott Winant	Nancy Oliver
10	"New World in My View"	Adam Davidson	Kate Barnow & Elisabeth R. Finch
11	"Frenzy"	Daniel Minahan	Alan Ball
12	"Beyond Here Lies Nothin'"	Michael Cuesta	Alexander Woo

Season Three

1	"Bad Blood"	Daniel Minahan	Brian Buckner
2	"Beautifully Broken"	Scott Winant	Raelle Tucker
3	"It Hurts Me Too"	Michael Lehmann	Alexander Woo
4	"9 Crimes"	David Petrarca	Barnow & Finch
5	"Trouble"	Scott Winant	Nancy Oliver
6	"I Got a Right to Sing the Blues"	Michael Lehmann	Alan Ball
7	"Hitting the Ground"	John Dahl	Brian Buckner
8	"Night on the Sun"	Lesli Linka Glatter	Raelle Tucker
9	"Everything Is Broken"	Scott Winant	Alexander Woo

10	"I Smell a Rat"	Michael Lehmann	Kate Barnow & Elisabeth R. Finch
11	"Fresh Blood"	Daniel Minahan	Nancy Oliver
12	"Evil Is Going On"	Anthony Hemingway	Alan Ball

Season 4

1	"She's Not There"	Michael Lehmann	Alexander Woo
2	"You Smell Like Dinner"	Scott Winant	Brian Buckner
3	"If You Love Me, Why Am I Dyin'?"	David Petrarca	Alan Ball
4	"I'm Alive and On Fire"	Michael Lehmann	Nancy Oliver
5	"Me and the Devil"	Daniel Minahan	Mark Hudis
6	"I Wish I Was the Moon"	Jeremy Podeswa	Raelle Tucker
7	"Cold Grey Light of Dawn"	Michael Ruscio	Alexander Woo
8	"Spellbound"	Daniel Minahan	Alan Ball
9	"Let's Get Out of Here"	Romeo Tirone	Brian Buckner
10	"Burning Down the House"	Lesli Linka Glatter	Nancy Oliver
11	"Soul of Fire"	Michael Lehmann	Mark Hudis
12	"And When I Die"	Scott Winant	Raelle Tucker

Season 5

1	"Turn! Turn! Turn!"	Daniel Minahan	Brian Buckner
2	"Authority Always Wins"	Michael Lehmann	Mark Hudis
3	"Whatever I Am, You Made Me"	David Petrarca	Raelle Tucker
4	"We'll Meet Again"	Romeo Tirone	Alexander Woo

5	"Let's Boot and Rally"	Michael Lehmann	Angela Robinson
6	"Hopeless"	Daniel Attias	Alan Ball
7	"In the Beginning"	Michael Ruscio	Brian Buckner
8	"Somebody That I Used to Know"	Stephen Moyer	Mark Hudis
9	"Everybody Wants to Rule the World"	Daniel Attias	Raelle Tucker
10	"Gone, Gone, Gone"	Scott Winant	Alexander Woo
11	"Sunset"	Lesli Linka Glatter	Angela Robinson
12	"Save Yourself"	Michael Lehmann	Alan Ball

Season 6

1	"Who Are You, Really?"	Stephen Moyer	Raelle Tucker
2	"The Sun"	Daniel Attias	Angela Robinson
3	"You're No Good"	Howard Deutch	Mark Hudis
4	"At Last"	Anthony Hemingway	Alexander Woo
5	"Fuck the Pain Away"	Michael Ruscio	Angela Robinson
6	"Don't You Feel Me?"	Howard Deutch	Daniel Kenneth
7	"In the Evening"	Scott Winant	Kate Barnow
8	"Dead Meat"	Michael Lehmann	Robin Veith
9	"Life Matters"	Romeo Tirone	Brian Buckner
10	"Radioactive"	Scott Winant	Kate Barnow

Booklist

1. *Dead Until Dark*
Sookie meets Bill in a nearly-identical plot to the show. Bill and Jason are both suspects in a series of local murders, including one that kills Adele. Sookie asks Bill to take her to Fangtasia, where she meets Eric and Pam. Eventually René is revealed as the murderer.

2. *Living Dead in Dallas*
Sookie is mysteriously attacked by a maenad (who doesn't feature heavily in the plot). Then she's enlisted to accompany Eric to Dallas to find a missing vampire. However, "Godfrey" is not Eric's saintly maker and Jason never joins the Fellowship of the Sun. Sookie sucks a bullet from Eric.

3. *Club Dead*
Lorena kidnaps Bill; Sookie enlists Alcide to track him down where he's held prisoner by the King of Mississippi, Russell Edgington (less of a villain in this version).

4. *Dead to the World*
The local witch coven gives Eric amnesia; he and Sookie fall in love. Jason is captured by the were panthers and changed into one of them.
- "Fairy Dust" in *A Touch of Dead*

- "Dracula Night" in *A Touch of Dead*

5. *Dead as a Doornail*
Shifters are being shot at, and Sookie's house is partially burned down, giving her a new mystery to solve. Sookie rescues Tara from her nasty vampire boyfriend and the were packs fight for a new leader.
- "One Word Answer" in *A Touch of Dead*

6. *Definitely Dead*
Sookie and her boyfriend Quinn the weretiger go to New Orleans to investigate her cousin Hadley's death.

7. *All Together Dead*
Katrina takes place. Sookie attends a vampire summit in the service of Queen Sophie-Anne. Amid vampire assassinations and attacks by the Church of the Sun, she and Barry the Bellboy publicly use their telepathy to become rescue workers.
- "Lucky" in *A Touch of Dead*

8. *From Dead to Worse*
Sookie meets her fairy great-grandfather Niall. There is a brief "war" between a New Orleans werewolf pack and the Alcide's Shreveport pack. Sookie is asked to arbitrate and keep everyone honest. Felipe de Castro, King of Nevada, attempts to take Louisiana from the injured Queen Sophie-Anne.
- "Gift Wrap" in *A Touch of Dead*

9. *Dead and Gone*
The shifter and were communities come out. Sookie investigates Crystal the were-panther's murder. The FBI is looking for Sookie to exploit her gifts. Eric finds a new way to establish Sookie as "his."
- "Two Blondes" in *Death's Excellent Vacation*

10. *Dead in the Family*
Eric's maker, Appius Livius Ocella, arrives with his unstable vampire child Alexei Romanov. Felipe de Castro's second, Victor Madden, abuses his power. Several lonely fairy relatives move in with Sookie.

- "Small-Town Wedding" in *The Sookie Stackhouse Companion*

11. *Dead Reckoning*
Sookie discovers the source of her telepathic abilities and finds a letter from her grandmother and a magical artifact. Sandra Pelt, Debbie's sister, plots against Sookie. Sookie and her friends deal with her and with Victor Madden.

12. *Deadlocked*
A murder takes place in Eric's house, and his relationship with Sookie begins to crumble. The fairies and Sam's were girlfriend Jannalynn plot against Sookie.

13. *Dead Ever After*
Sookie is arrested for murder herself, and discovers what the town really thinks of her. Sam has a secret. At last, Sookie decides whom she wants to spend her life with. Around her, most of her friends marry, have babies, and otherwise settle down.

- "If I Had A Hammer" in *Home Improvement: Undead Edition*

- "Playing Possum" in *An Apple for the Creature*

Also recommended

Sookie Stackhouse Books
  After Dead: What Came Next in the World of Sookie Stackhouse
  The Sookie Stackhouse Companion (interviews and guide)
  A Touch of Dead (short story collection)

True Blood Books
The *True Blood* Graphic Novels
  True Blood Volume 1: All Together Now
  True Blood Volume 2: Tainted Love
  True Blood Volume 3: The French Quarter
  True Blood Volume 4: Where Were You?

True Blood Volume 5: Shake For Me
True Blood Volume 6: Here We Go Again

True Blood: Eats, Drinks, and Bites from Bon Temps. (cookbook by show creators)
Steve Newlin's Field Guide to Vampires (guide from the show creators, coming November 2013)

Works Cited

Ball, Alan. Commentary 1.1, "Strange Love." *True Blood: The Complete First Season.* HBO Home Entertainment, 2009. DVD.

Brick, Emily. "True Blood, Sex and Online Fan Culture." Glynn, Aston, and Johnson 47-62.

Brinton, Daniel G. *Nagualism: A Study in Native American Folk-lore and History.* 2008. EBook #26426. http://www.gutenberg.org/files/26426/26426-0.txt

Buchanan, Kyle. "The Verge: Rutina Wesley." *Movieline.* 1 June 2009. http://movieline.com/2009/06/01/the-verge-rutina-wesley.

Buckner, Brian. "Inside the Episode" "You Smell Like Dinner." *True Blood: The Complete Fourth Season.* HBO Home Entertainment, 2012. DVD.

Buttsworth, Sara. "Cinderbella: Twilight, Fairy Tales, and the Twenty-First Century American Dream." *Twilight and History,* ed. Nancy R. Reagin. Hoboken, NJ: John Wiley & Sons, 2010. 47-69.

Campbell, Joseph. *The Hero with a Thousand Faces.* New York: Princeton University Press, 1973.

Campbell, Joseph, and Bill Moyers, *The Power of Myth.* Ed. Betty Sue Flowers. New York: Doubleday, 1988.

Carr, Coeli. "Real Witches Cry Foul at Portrayal on 'True Blood.'" *Reuters Canada.* 12 Aug 2011. http://ca.reuters.com/article/entertainmentNews/idCATR E77B54Q20110812?sp=true.

Carroll, Noël. *The Philosophy of Horror or Paradoxes of the Heart.*

New York: Routledge, 1990.

Cashdan, Sheldon. *The Witch Must Die*. New York: Basic Books, 1999.

"Catemaco Brujos." 2013. http://www.catemaco.info/brujos.

Cherry, Brigid, ed. *True Blood: Investigating Vampires and Southern Gothic*. New York: I.B. Tauris, 2012.

Condis, Megan Amber. "Ghosts between the Pages: The Devolution of Medb from Sovereignty Goddess to Comic Book Villainess and the Potential Dangers of the Transcription of Oral Tales." *The International Journal of the Book* 7:2. (2010).

Corn, Kevin J. and George A. Dunn. "Let the Bon Temps Roll: Sacrifice, Scapegoats, and Good Times." Dunn and Housel 139-156.

Craton, Lillian E. and Kathryn E. Jonell. "I am Sookie. Hear Me Roar: Sookie Stackhouse and Feminist Ambivalence." Dunn and Housel 109-122.

Crook, John. "'True Blood's' Rutina Wesley: In Season 6, 'all hell is breaking loose'" 16 June 2013. http://blog.zap2it.com/frominsidethebox/2013/06/true-blood-makes-an-action-packed-return-to-hbo.html.

Cuesta, Michael and Alexander Woo. Commentary, "Beyond Here Lies Nothin'," *True Blood: The Complete Second Season*. HBO Home Entertainment, 2010. DVD.

Curran, Bob. *Encyclopedia of the Undead*. New Jersey: New Page Books, 2006.

Downing, Christine. "Sisters and Brothers." Downing, 110–17.

—. ed. *Mirrors of the Self: Archetypal Images that Shape Your Life*. New York: St. Martin's Press, 1991.

Dunn, George A. and Rebecca Housel, eds. *True Blood and Philosophy*. USA: Blackwell, 2010.

Estés, Clarissa Pinkola. *Women Who Run With the Wolves*. New York: Ballantine Books, 1992.

Euripides. *The Bacchae*. Trans. Gilbert Murray. USA: Project Gutenberg, 2011. http://www.gutenberg.org/files/35173/35173-h/35173-h.htm.

Evans-Wentz, W.Y. *The Fairy-Faith in Celtic Countries. London and*

New York: H. Froude, 1911. *The Sacred Texts Archive*. http://www.sacred-texts.com/neu/celt/ffcc/ffcc121.htm

"Exclusive: Stephen King on J.K. Rowling, Stephenie Meyer." *USA Weekend* 2 Feb. 2009. http://whosnews.usaweekend.com/2009/02/exclusiv e-stephen-king-on-jk-rowling-stephenie-meyer.

"First Draft: Vampire Sookie." "Somebody That I Used to Know." *True Blood: The Complete Fifth Season*. HBO Go. 2012. Online Television. http://www.hbogo.com/

Fordham, Michael. *Jungian Psychotherapy*. USA: Avon, 1978.

Frankel, Valerie Estelle. *Buffy and the Heroine's Journey*. Jefferson, NC: McFarland and Co., 2012.

—. *From Girl to Goddess: The Heroine's Journey through Myth and Legend*. Jefferson, NC: McFarland and Co., 2010.

—. *The Many Faces of Katniss Everdeen: Exploring the Heroine of The Hunger Games*. USA: Winged Lion Press, 2013.

Gaines, Janet Howe. "Lilith: Seductress, Heroine or Murderer?" *Bible History Daily*. 4 Sept 2012 http://www.biblicalarchaeology.org/daily/people-cultures-in-the-bible/people-in-the-bible/lilith/

Garry, Jane and Hasan El-Shamy. "The Trickster." *Archetypes & Motifs in Folklore & Literature: A Handbook*. USA: M.E. Sharpe, 2005, 472-480.

Gaster, Moses. "Two Thousand Years of a Charm against the Child-Stealing Witch." *Folk-Lore* Vol 11, London: The Folk Lore Society, 1900. 129-161.

Glynn, Basil, James Aston, and Beth Johnson, eds. *Television, Sex, and Society: Analyzing Contemporary Representations*. New York: Continuum, 2012.

Guiley, Rosemary Ellen. *The Complete Vampire Companion*. New York: Macmillan, 1994.

—. *The Encyclopedia of Vampires and Werewolves*. USA: Visionary Living, 2011.

Halterman, Jim. "Kristin Bauer Teases True Blood Season 6, Changing Pam and Eric Relationship." *TV Fanatic*. June 13, 2013. http://www.tvfanatic.com/2013/06/kristin-bauer-teases-true-blood-season-6-changing-pam-and-eric-r/

Harris, Charlaine. "Charlaine Harris Answers Questions from

her Fans." *The Sookie Stackhouse Companion* 301-312.

—. *All Together Dead*. New York: Ace Books, 2010.

—. *Club Dead*. New York: Ace Books, 2009.

—. *Dead as a Doornail*. New York: Ace Books, 2006.

—. *Dead Ever After*. New York: Penguin, 2013.

—. *Deadlocked*. New York: Penguin, 2012.

—. "Dracula Night." *A Touch of Dead* 35-72.

—. *From Dead to Worse*. New York: Ace Books, 2008.

—. "One-Word Answer." *A Touch of Dead* 73-112

—. "Small Town Wedding" *The Sookie Stackhouse Companion*. 1-80.

—. *The Sookie Stackhouse Companion*. USA: Penguin, 2011.

—. *A Touch of Dead*. USA: Penguin, 2009.

Hirschbein, Ron. "Sookie, Sigmund, and the Edible Complex." Dunn and Housel 123-138.

Hyde, Lewis. *Trickster Makes This World*. New York: Farrar, Straus, and Giroux, 1998.

Kaveney, Roz, ed. *Reading the Vampire Slayer: The Unofficial Critical Companion to Buffy and Angel*. USA: Tauris Parke, 2002.

Kenneth, Daniel and Howard Deutch. "Inside the Episode." "Don't You Feel Me." *True Blood: The Complete Sixth Season*. HBO Go. 2013. Online Television. http://www.hbogo.com/

Keveney, Bill, "'True Blood' Sinks its Teeth into Politics for Fifth Season." *USA Today* 8 June 2012. http://usatoday30.usatoday.com/life/television/news/story/2012-06-07/true-blood-season-5/55447106/1.

—. "HBO's 'True Blood' Going Back to its Roots. *USA Today* 21 July 2013. http://www.usatoday.com/story/life/tv/2013/07/20/true-blood-shows-its-fangs-at-comic-con/2571957/

Laycock, Joseph. "Rights, and the Political Underpinnings of HBO's True Blood" *Religion and Politics Fit for Polite Company*. A Project of the John C. Danforth Center on Religion & Politics Washington University in St. Louis. 27 August 2012. http://religionandpolitics.org/2012/08/27/vampires-gay-rights-and-the-political-underpinnings-of-hbos-true-blood.

Leon, Hilary M. "Why We Love the Monsters: How Anita Blake, Vampire Hunter, and Buffy the Vampire Slayer Wound Up Dating the Enemy." *Slayage* 1.1 http://slayageonline.com/PDF/leon.pdf

Lima, Maria. "Home Is Where the Bar Is." Wilson 33-44.

Maberry, Jonathan and Janice Gable Bashman. *Wanted Undead or Alive: Vampire Hunters and Other Kick-Ass Enemies of Evil.* USA: Citadel, 2010.

Mack, Carol K. and Dinah. *A Field Guide to Demons, Vampires, Fallen Angels and Other Subversive Spirits.* USA: Skyhorse, 2011.

Mamatas, Nick. "Working Class Heroes: The Blue-Collar Politics of True Blood." Wilson 61-74.

Marshall, Richard. *Witchcraft: The History and Mythology.* New York: Crescent Books, 1995.

Martin, Michael. "Anna Paquin." *Interview Magazine.* 2013. http://www.interviewmagazine.com/film/anna-paquin-true-blood.

McClelland, Bruce A. "Un-True Blood: The Politics of Artificiality." Dunn and Housel 79-92.

Miller, Mary and Karl Taube. *The Gods and Symbols of Ancient Mexico and the Maya: An Illustrated Dictionary of Mesoamerican Religion.* London: Thames & Hudson, 1993.

Monaghan, Patricia. *The New Book of Goddesses and Heroines.* St. Paul, Minnesota: Llewellyn Publications, 1997.

Mukherjea, Ananaya. "Characters and Identities Mad, Bad and Delectable to Know: True Blood's Paranormal Men and Gothic Romance" Cherry 109-121.

Mullins, Jenna. "True Blood Season 6: Everything We Know About What Lies Ahead." June 17, 2013. http://www.eonline.com/news/430575/true-blood-season-6-everything-we-know-about-what-lies-ahead

O'Connor, Mickey. "True Blood's Michelle Forbes Ponders 'The Riddle of Maryann.'" *TVGuide.com* Jul 11, 2009 http://www.tvguide.com/News/True-Blood-Forbes-1007941.aspx.

Pearson, Carol, and Katherine Pope. *The Female Hero in American and British Literature.* New York: R.R. Bowker, 1981.

Peppers-Bates, Susan and Joshua Rust. "A Vampire's Heart Has

Its Reasons That Scientific Naturalism Can't Understand." Dunn and Housel 187-202.

Perera, Silvia Brinton. *Descent to the Goddess*. Toronto: Inner City Books, 1981.

Playden, Zoe-Jane. "What You Are, What's to Come: Feminisms, Citizenship, and the Divine." Kaveney 120-147.

Poole, Carol. "The Ego, the Id, and Sookie Stackhouse. True Blood's Freudian Analysis of Intimacy." Wilson 75-88.

Pritchett, Jeffery. "Navajo Skinwalkers and Legends' Interview w/ J.C. Johnson of Crypto Four Corners." *The Examiner.* May 4, 2012 http://www.examiner.com/article/navajo-skinwalkers-and-legends-interview-w-jc-johnson-of-crypto-four-corners

"The Real Salome." "Somebody That I Used to Know." *True Blood: The Complete Fifth Season.* HBO Go. 2012. Online Television. http://www.hbogo.com/

Rubin, Jonna. "SOOKEH! Bee-ill! and the Downfall of William T. Compton: How Vampire Bill Went From Sex Symbol to Sad Punchline." Wilson 19-32.

Ruddell, Caroline and Brigid Cherry "More than Cold and Heartless: The Southern Gothic Milieu of True Blood" Cherry 39-58.

Sayer, Karen. "It Wasn't Our World Anymore. They Made it Theirs: Reading Space and Place." Kaveney 98-119.

Senf, Carol A. *The Vampire in Nineteenth Century English Literature.* USA: Popular Press, 1988.

Shakespeare, William. *The Riverside Shakespeare*, 2nd ed. Boston: Houghton Mifflin, 1997.

Shepherd, Rowena and Rupert. *1000 Symbols*. New York: The Ivy Press, 2002.

"Smashed" *Buffy the Vampire Slayer. The Complete Sixth Season.* UPN. 2001-2002. DVD. Los Angeles: 20th Century Fox, 2004.

Sobol, Gianna and Alan Ball with Karen Sommer Shalett. *True Blood: Eats, Drinks, and Bites from Bon Temps.* USA: Chronicle Books, 2012.

Steiger, Brad. *Real Vampires, Night Stalkers, and Creatures from the Darkside.* USA: Visible Ink Press, 2010.

——. *The Werewolf Book: The Encyclopedia of Shape-Shifting Beings.* USA: Visible Ink Press, 2011

Stern, David and Mirsky, Mark Jay. *Rabbinic Fantasies: Imaginative Narratives from Classical Hebrew Literature* (Yale Judaica Series). Philadelphia, Jewish Publication Society, 1990.

Summers, Montague. *The Vampire, His Kith and Kin.* New York, E.P. Dutton & Co., 1929. The Sacred Texts Archive. http://www.sacred-texts.com/goth/vkk/vkk00.htm.

True Blood: The Complete First Season. HBO Home Entertainment, 2009. DVD.

True Blood: The Complete Fifth Season. HBO Go. 2012. Online Television. http://www.hbogo.com.

True Blood: The Complete Fourth Season. HBO Home Entertainment, 2012. DVD.

True Blood: The Complete Second Season. HBO Home Entertainment, 2010. DVD.

True Blood: The Complete Sixth Season. HBO Go. 2013. Online Television. http://www.hbogo.com.

True Blood: The Complete Third Season. HBO Home Entertainment, 2011. DVD.

Tucker, Raelle. "Inside the Episodes: Episode 12: And When I Die." *True Blood: The Complete Fourth Season.* HBO Go. 2011. Online Television. http://www.hbogo.com.

Tyley, Jodie. "Charlaine Harris on After Dead and Midnight Crossroad." *SciFiNow.* 17 July 2013. http://www.scifinow.co.uk/news/46212/charlaine-harris-on-after-dead-and-post-sookie-series-midnight-crossroads/

——. "Charlaine Harris on Death Threats and Dead Ever After." *SciFiNow.* 18 July 2013. http://www.scifinow.co.uk/news/46316/charlaine-harris-on-death-threats-and-dead-ever-after

——. "True Blood Books: Who Will Sookie End Up With?" *SciFiNow.* 30 January 2013. http://www.scifinow.co.uk/interviews/35263/true-blood-books-who-will-sookie-end-up-with

Vogler, Christopher. *The Writer's Journey.* USA: Michael Wiese Productions, 1998.

Von Franz, Marie-Louise. *The Feminine in Fairy Tales.* Boston: Shambhala, 1993.

Walker, Barbara G. *The Woman's Dictionary of Symbols and Sacred Objects.* San Francisco: Harper, 1988.

Waltje, Jörg. *Blood Obsession: Vampires, Serial Murder, and the Popular Imagination.* New York: Peter Lang Publishing, 2005.

Waters, Melanie. "Fangbanging: Sexing the Vampire in Alan Ball's *True Blood.*" Glynn, Aston, and Johnson 33-46.

Wesley, Rutina. "Vamp Vindication" "Somebody That I Used to Know" *True Blood: The Complete Fifth Season.* HBO Go. 2012. Online Television. http://www.hbogo.com/

Wigington, Patti. "Basic Principles and Concepts of Wicca." *About.com Guide.* http://paganwiccan.about.com.

Wilcott, Becca. *Truly, Madly, Deadly: The Unofficial True Blood Companion.* USA: ECW Press, 2010.

Wilde, Lady Francesca Speranza. *Ancient Legends, Mystic Charms, and Superstitions of Ireland.* London: Ward & Downey, 1887. *The Sacred Texts Archive.* http://www.sacred-texts.com/neu/celt/ali/ali000.htm

Wilson, Leah, ed. *A Taste of True Blood: The Fangbanger's Guide.* USA: BenBella Books, Inc. 2010.

Wisker, Gina. "Vampires and School Girls: High School Jinks on the Hellmouth," *Slayage* 1.2 (March 2001). http://slayageonline.com/PDF/wisker.pdf.

Wloszczyna, Susan. "Classic Romantic Triangle Takes Monstrous Form in 'New Moon'." *USA Today* 15 Nov. 2009. http://abcnews.go.com/Entertainment/love-triangle-looms-twilights-moon/story?id=9076121#.UDPa191lRn8.

Woll, Deborah Ann. Commentary, "You Smell Like Dinner." *True Blood: The Complete Fourth Season.* HBO Home Entertainment, 2012. DVD.

Zweig, Connie. "The Conscious Feminine: Birth of a New Archetype," Downing, 183–91.

Index

BLOODSUCKERS ON THE BAYOU

About the Author

Valerie Estelle Frankel is the author of many nonfiction books:

- ❖ *Buffy and the Heroine's Journey*
- ❖ *From Girl to Goddess: The Heroine's Journey in Myth and Legend*
- ❖ *Katniss the Cattail: An Unauthorized Guide to Names and Symbols in The Hunger Games*
- ❖ *The Many Faces of Katniss Everdeen: Exploring the Heroine of The Hunger Games*
- ❖ *Harry Potter, Still Recruiting: An Inner Look at Harry Potter Fandom*
- ❖ *Teaching with Harry Potter*
- ❖ *Myths and Motifs in The Mortal Instruments*
- ❖ *Winter is Coming: Symbols, Portents, and Hidden Meanings in A Game of Thrones*
- ❖ *Winning the Game of Thrones: The Host of Characters and their Agendas*

Once a lecturer at San Jose State University, she's a frequent speaker on fantasy, myth, pop culture, and the heroine's journey and can be found at http://vefrankel.com.

www.ingramcontent.com/pod-product-compliance
Lightning Source LLC
Chambersburg PA
CBHW021151020426
42331CB00003B/13